Life-Cycle Ceremonies

Also available from the Celebrant Foundation and Institute:
*Stories from Funeral Celebrants: Celebrating
the Life While Mourning the Death*

Foundation & Institute

Life-Cycle Ceremonies:
A Handbook for Your Whole Life

Co-edited by Sheri Reda and Charlotte Eulette

Introduction by Sheri Reda
Foreward by Charlotte Eulette, CF&I International Director

Design by Sarah Lemp

Printed in the United States of America.

A Celebrant Foundation and Institute Publication
93 Valley Road, 2nd Floor, Montclair, NJ 07042.

www.celebrantinstitute.org
information@celebrantinstitute.org
Fax: 973.746.1775 Telephone: 973.746.1792

Publisher's Cataloging-in-Publication Data
Life-cycle ceremonies: a handbook for your whole life / 1st ed.
Compiled and Edited by Sheri Reda and Charlotte Eulette
Graphic Design by Sarah Lemp
p. cm.

Includes bibliographical references.

ISBN 978-0-9904406-0-4 (pbk)
ISBN 978-0-9904406-1-1 (epub)
ISBN 978-0-9904406-2-8 (mobi)

1.Rites and Ceremonies – 2. Self-Realization – 3. New Careers -
4. Career Changes – 5. Celebrant -6. Celebrant Foundation & Institute
7. Personal Awareness and Self-Improvement – 8. Reference, general.
GN473 .L544 2014
Dewey Class Number 390

First Printing, 2015

14 13 12 11 10 / 10 9 8 7 6 5 4 3 2 1

*We send out love and gratitude to Gaile Sarma and Pat Sarma,
who established the Celebrant Foundation & Institute;
Dally Messenger III, the father-of-invention and
Principal of the International College of Celebrancy;
our DPA colleagues, along with Frank A. Reda, Sr.;
and all Life-Cycle Celebrants who do this important work.*

Thank you!

Table of Contents

Foreword

The beautifully effective ceremonies on these pages are pre-tested and approved methods for setting aside ordinary time and sitting, standing, walking, dancing in awareness.

They help us honor the moments, the seasons, the losses, the experiences that invite our awareness. Some of them are designed for daily use, to support and sustain a personal practice. Others offer a way to witness personal transitions or honor natural cycles of birth, growth, death, and transformation. I am happy to endorse each and every one.

You can use these ceremonies as blueprints to follow, step-by-step, or you can improvise upon them to create one-of-a-kind ceremonies with personal resonance. You can also use them as a guide to the rites you want to include in a celebrant-led ceremony. These are boons we share with you as we all continue to journey toward wholeness.

– Charlotte Eulette,
International Director
Celebrant Foundation & Institution

Acknowledgment

The ceremonies that comprise this book have been freely offered by certified Life-Cycle Celebrants® who are graduates of the Celebrant Foundation and Institute.

About the Celebrant Foundation & Institute

Founded in 2001 by philanthropists Gaile and Pat Sarma as an educational non-profit headquartered in Montclair, New Jersey, the Celebrant Foundation and Institute (CF&I) is the nation's preeminent online educational institute for teaching and certifying modern day ritual and ceremony professionals, or Life-Cycle Celebrants.® Through CF&I's seven-month, web-based educational program, students are rigorously schooled in the art of ritual, ceremony, world and faith traditions, mythology, ceremonial writing, and public speaking. They learn to officiate at virtually every life event and to focus on strategies for personalizing each ceremony to reflect the needs, beliefs, and values of the individual, couple, or family. Celebrant-led ceremonies by CF&I graduates honor weddings, civil unions, funerals, baby and child arrivals, and myriad other events honoring the milestones and important moments in people's lives.

A member of the International Federation of Celebrants, CF&I has graduated more than 1,000 Life-Cycle Celebrants® who preside over 30,000 ceremonies each year. They practice their craft throughout the entire world. Their numbers grow yearly, as do the scope and influence of their ceremonies.

To learn more about the Celebrant Foundation & Institute, please visit the website, www.celebrantinstitute.org.

About Life-Cycle Celebrants®

Life-Cycle Celebrants® are certified graduates of the Celebrant Foundation & Institute whose ceremonies mark personal and professional milestones in people's lives. They officiate at virtually every life event, with a focus on personalizing each ceremony to reflect the needs, beliefs, and values of their clients.

Introduction

Our lives are inherently meaningful. Whether we notice it or not, we engage every day in the world around us. We balance the past and the present, enter into relationships with friends and strangers, and seek within ourselves and others a store of wisdom from which to act.

Every moment of our engagement brings conflict between what we know or guess we know and what we actually experience. Sometimes what we experience is far, far happier than what we thought we knew to expect. Sometimes it's challenging or troubling or traumatic. For better or worse, however, every act (or decision not to act) brings new experience, and every new experience carries a loss of innocence. Thus we emerge from every moment both richer and poorer, and irreversibly changed. That's why celebrants talk about life events in terms of the hero's journey.

In his book *The Hero With a Thousand Faces*, Joseph Campbell popularized the idea of the hero's journey by summarizing and analyzing the recurrent theme in mythology and legend:

> A hero ventures forth from the world of common day into
> a region of supernatural wonder: fabulous forces are there
> encountered and a decisive victory is won: the hero comes
> back from this mysterious adventure with the power to
> bestow boons on his fellow man.

Campbell was mostly concerned with those extraordinary moments in life—birth, coming of age, marriage, death—that mark the large transitions we make from one stage of life to another. However, every day is drenched in the extraordinary, though we are mostly too busy to perceive it all. Every day is a challenge to our equilibrium, and every day we are able to emerge with another sliver of wisdom.

It can be comforting to think that we are all embarked upon a continual hero's journey toward wholeness. It puts us where we belong, in the starring role in our own lives. It lends sobriety to our struggles and nobility to our goals. But the hero's journey is daunting, as well. If we are heroes, and on a quest, does that mean we can fail? Can one fail at life?

The disconcerting short answer is *yes*. We can fail in both greater and lesser ways. The failure we fear, however, is paradoxically a lesser failure: we fear we will fail to meet our goals, fulfill our quests, and change the world in the ways we envision. That kind of failure is merely personal failure. It's the failure of Thomas Edison, who made at least a thousand unsuccessful attempts before he succeeded in inventing the light bulb. Or Vincent Van Gogh, who sold only one painting during his lifetime and died never knowing that he had forever changed the word of art. Or Odysseus, that legendary hero whose failure to return home for twenty years was part of the world's greatest epic. Personal failure is painful, but it's far from a referendum on our contributions. In fact, it's a given part of the hero's journey.

A greater failure lies in sidestepping any significant engagement with the world. In other words, we may fear failure. And we may, on some levels, fail. But the only positive choice is to engage, and by engaging we always—yes, always—win. We deepen our experience of the world to include perspectives outside our own. We encounter ourselves and others as actors in the great drama of life. And we lose innocence but gain experience, which is the boon we share, the gift we give the world. That is, in a nutshell, the heroic condition, the condition by which we are all heroes, not only in our own lives but also in the wider world. This in itself is something to celebrate; we are always heroes and always either home or on our way. Ceremonies to celebrate the moments in this journey are salutary in that they acknowledge our struggles, sustain our efforts, console us in our losses, and celebrate our victories, large and small. Performing ceremonies brings us that boon of hard-won wisdom we gain from living our lives.

As the anthropologist Victor Turner noted in his book *From Ritual to Theatre*, the word perform derives from the French *parfournir*, which means "to complete," or "to carry out thoroughly." Ceremony is a performance that binds the past to the eternal present. It completes an event, incorporating it into the body of lived experience. To perform a ceremony, then, is to give an event or a moment or a hard-won gem of wisdom its utmost expression. The act of performing a ceremony integrates whatever you choose to celebrate or commemorate into your overall story, forging it into a tool for access to your storehouse of personal wisdom. This is the source of my own passion for ceremonies.

As a child in the 1960s and '70s, I experienced both the powerful efficacy and the stifling sense of a straightjacket in timeworn Italian customs and traditional Roman Catholic canons. On one hand, I cherished the sense of belonging that came with mass and Sunday dinner at my grandmother's house. On the other, I sought relief from the unilateral characterization that my religion, ethnicity, and immediate family imposed upon my sense of identity. I knew I was more and less and different than the person my church and family understood me to be.

I relished the sense of sanctuary created by Catholic ritual. Yet I found at last that I couldn't pay the entry fee of strict adherence to a dogma that didn't fit. Like the hippies just ahead of me, I undertook a wholesale rejection of anything that smacked of tradition, and that was fun for a while, but it left me without a foundation from which to build. So I began the painstaking progress of constructing a new foundation, a structure that reflected my experience and study and the values to which I dedicate my life.

I found one cornerstone of my new foundation through a conscious commitment to love—personal, social, and spiritual love—as the guiding principle for my life. I found another in writing, creating forms out of the amorphous universe of thought, sensibility, and experience. I shaped a third through theater and performance. By constructing or collaborating on the construction of experiential realities, I felt I was helping to create and share entire worlds of possibility. I found the fourth cornerstone in seminary, where I explored the fundamental search for truth that is both the source of all religion and the reason why communities of faith and communities of commitment can thrive.

These cornerstones, combined with action and reflection, helped me build a new foundation from which to engage in the world humbly, authentically, and in sync with my values. The synergy between them assuaged my hunger for heightened experience and my thirst for a higher consciousness. And the structure that resulted seems to be able to bear a lot of weight. Though I don't always trust it as I might, it has supported years of seeking and finding and storing and losing and re-encountering experiential wisdom. It's justified lots of jobs and creative experimentation and episodes of collaboration with wise people like me, and fools like me, and people who don't seem at first to be at all like me.

In 2011, this synergy led me to the Celebrant Foundation and Institute (CF&I), where I learned to codify my experience and knowledge and collaborate with other celebrants, emerging heroically with certifications in Weddings, Funerals, Ceremonies Across the Life Cycle, and Ceremonies for Healing. In the process, I have lost some innocence (or ignorance) about the deep changes that transform us during milestone events and also on a day-to-day basis. I've gained experiential awe regarding the human experience—the hero's journey.

I am honored to have collected and organized these ceremonies, along with Charlotte Eulette, on behalf of CF&I, which trains and supports some of the world's most prolific and effective Life-Cycle Celebrants®. Special thanks to Gale Sarma and Pat Sarma, our visionary and dedicated founders, and also to Charlotte, the International Director, whose generosity of spirit infuses CF&I and its projects with energy and warmth. Thanks also to Rhiannon Koehler and Alexandra Lifshin for their editorial skills, Kim Kirkley, who served as our publishing mentor and guru, and the Life-Cycle Celebrants®who contributed to this collection. To all those who help bring out the meaning in everyday life—enjoy!

– Sheri Reda

"Wisdom sits in places"

— Apache proverb

CHAPTER 1
Ceremonial Space

You may have noticed the way snow on the ground softens the harsh lines of winter. The way autumn leaves offer a consoling whisper when they rustle. The way that organizing your space can sharpen your thoughts, galvanize your intentions, and make the previously impossible into something plausible. Even the places you make for yourself become special over time. Your office or den can be a sanctuary. Your kitchen becomes the safe place for confidences over coffee klatch. Your bedroom is the place where you recharge, emerging each day with new energy and strength.

All these experiences speak to the connection between place and person. They demonstrate that every place is sacred space! Some places, like the Grand Canyon or Niagara Falls, plainly demonstrate their overwhelming natural power. Others, like a spot in the woods or the bank of a winding creek, simply draw us into their quiet strength. Still others reveal their power progressively, as we invest in them. Labyrinths, gardens, backyards, and living room altars each reveal their special nature over time.

Connecting with the energy of a place can offer us succor and strength, and that's where the following ceremonies come in. Amy Benedict and Jeff Wallis offer ways to trace the lines of the sacred in your neighborhood. Carolyn Niethammer offers a humble way to harvest nature's goodness. Deborah Belaus finds a way to weather the weather in peace. Charlotte Eulette demonstrates the restorative power of the labyrinth, and Kevin O'Brien offers a way to bring the peace of one place into your larger life.

These ceremonies are suggestive of the many ways you can add inspiration to the all-important moments that make up every day. Whether you incorporate them into your daily practice or use them to set the tone for larger celebrations, they promise to evoke a sense of sanctuary.

A Neighborhood Pilgrimage

AMY BENEDICT

A pilgrimage is a journey of great moral or spiritual significance. With that in mind, take a walk in your neighborhood with intention and new awareness. Open yourself to a universe of possibilities. A simple walk from home and back can become a ritual to enact the sacred quest that is life.

MATERIALS

Wear comfortable clothes that make it easy to move. Consider whether to blend in with your surroundings or add a bit of color and personal expression.

PREPARATION

Acknowledge all that you are leaving behind as you step across the threshold of your home into the out-of-doors. Mindfully, let it go.

THE WALK

You have left home, yet you are not going on to any particular destination. Your pilgrimage is a search for poetry, and it's up to you to imbue it with meaning.

- Consciously open yourself to the mystery and wonder that lies before you. If it is a sunny day, observe the play of light and shadow. Notice the rhythm of your gait in relation to the expansion and contraction of your breath. Feel the subtle warming exertion of moving your body. Observe the movement, of other beings, of cars and clouds.

- Experience all the ways in which you are a part of this dance of creatures, architecture, vehicles, and the natural landscape.

- Consider the shape of your route from a bird's eye view. Your walk may take you alongside roads or down sidewalks. You may find yourself walking a path formed by others' footsteps around or beside a body of water, a woods, or a field. Contemplate these intersections of nature and human consciousness. Maybe you'll find a symbolic object (a stone, pine cone, an event flyer, a coin, a budding branch).

- Be aware of both what you are taking in and what you offer as you meet this familiar world anew. Cultivate curiosity and feelings of gratitude.

IN CLOSING

As you cross the threshold into your home again, think about the perspectives and discoveries you are bringing with you upon your return. To process your experience, write poetry or prose. Draw or paint. Compose or play music. Or simply sip a beverage and revel in the quiet transformation your pilgrimage has wrought.

AMY BENEDICT is a Life-Cycle Celebrant® with certification in Weddings and Ceremonies Across the Life Cycle. She makes her home in the Hudson Valley of New York. Amy can be reached by email at marigoldceremonies@gmail.com or through her website, www.marigoldceremonies.com.

Finding Spirit In Leaves & Berries

CAROLYN NIETHAMMER

I must have been about five years old when I asked my mom why Grandpa didn't go to church with us. "He says he goes to church in his garden," was her reply. Many decades passed, and I had forgotten about her answer until I realized that I was doing the same thing. I am never so happy or peaceful or connected to the oneness of all than when I am in my garden or gathering foods from the wild.

MATERIALS

For gardening: I love working compost and fertilizer into the soil around my vegetables and ornamental plants. I balance the nutrients, plant the seeds, and wait for the creative power of the universe to push up the first tiny green sprouts.

For gathering: What a pleasure to assemble gathering tools—tongs, poles, and baskets—and go into the desert to gather the foods growing there.

PREPARATION

To harvest your local resources, learn when and where they ripen into fullness. My local treasures include the saguaro cactus. Saguaro cacti are the tall plants with many arms so iconic of the American Southwest. People of the Tohono O'odham Nation, who live on the desert's bounty, traditionally started their year with the saguaro harvest. Saguaros produce fruit in late June when temperatures can soar far above 100 in the middle of the day. To get my share, I get up before dawn to drive to the desert and collect in the cooler early morning.

THE GATHERING

- Walk out among the plants you plan to harvest.

- Acknowledge your fellow living beings. Alone with the plants, my only companions the doves and other birds looking for a saguaro fruit breakfast, I find myself talking to the saguaros. "So what have you got for me?" I'll ask.

- Maneuvering the rocky hills is strenuous, so when one plant contributes several fat, perfectly ripe fruits, I always say thank you.

IN CLOSING

By growing a garden and collecting berries or wild greens or cactus fruits, we can connect spiritually with our mother, the abundant Earth, and remind ourselves of our place in the universe.

CAROLYN NIETHAMMER is a Life-Cycle Celebrant® with certification in Weddings and Funerals. Carolyn lives in Tucson with her husband. She can be reached by email at carolyn@cniethammer.com or through her website, www.ceremoniesofdistinction.com.

Connecting Nature with the Human Spirit

DEBORAH BELAUS

In the past few years, Earth has been acquainting us with extreme weather. When the power goes out, we are forced into opportunities we often overlook: to connect with neighbors, play with children, and read the books that have been piling up on the shelves. And when the lights come back on, you can retain the benefits of simplicity using a nature ceremony to stay grounded and healthy.

PREPARATION

- Begin making sure that wherever you decide to step out, you feel safe.

- Before taking a step, take three deep breaths and listen to the sounds that surround you. As you breathe in, take in the smells that surround you. As you breathe out, notice the feel and temperature of the air that surrounds you.

- Without judgment ask yourself, *how does my physical body feel?*

- Without judgment ask yourself, *what mood am I in?*

- Set an intention for your walk and ask nature for guidance to help you find clarity.

THE CONNECTING

- As you walk, look for symbolism in everything that surrounds you. A tall, strong tree can give you inspiration to stand on your own two feet. Perhaps an uprooted tree will give you insight to how you are feeling or the gifts you can give. The simplicity of a dewdrop touching a flower might help you ease into calmness. Looking up at the sky could allow your mind to reach for new possibilities.

- Along the way pick up items that will remind you of your experience, items you can place somewhere in your home to inspire you to walk again.

- Before you go back indoors again, find yourself in the flow of unspoken communication: Listen!

IN CLOSING

Create from your metaphors a new sense of purpose. Mother Nature is a good, solid therapist. She will lead you to yourself and help answer your questions. And the consultation is free of charge!

DEBORAH BELAUS is a Life-Cycle Celebrant® with certification in Weddings. Deborah lives in Rhode Island. She can be reached by email at adeborahbelaus@gmail.com or through her website, www.brightpathceremonies.com.

Memory Walk

JEFF WALLIS

The restorative power of nature can be accessible anytime, anywhere, through the ritual of a memory walk.

MATERIALS
- Camera
- Walking path or route

PREPARATION

The Plan: Pick a five-to-ten-minute route that comforts or captivates you...or find a new one. Explore local trails or identify a new stretch of beach or woods.

`The Initial Walk: Pause at the beginning point for a minute, and also at four or five additional points along the way. Use all your senses to feel where you are.

- Take note of prominent landmarks or plants. Listen to the sounds that fill the area. Smell the air. Store the sensations as sensory markers to recall later.

- Pause to take a few photographs at each of these "sensory spots."

THE MEMORY WALK

Now imbue this life experience with meaning.

- Set aside a spot, such as favorite chair, from which to embark on your memory walk.

- Find a comfortable position and close your eyes. Take several deep breaths to relax and focus.

- Recall the sights, sounds, smells, and sensations of the walk. Capture with your mind's eye each picture that you took with your camera, or call up on your computer a slideshow of your walk.

IN CLOSING

I take a memory walk several times each week. I also have several walks stored for recall, including one in my neighborhood, one from a nature trail, and another along a beautiful Caribbean beach. The ritual of taking a memory walk gives me unlimited access to the calming and restorative powers of nature.

JEFF WALLIS is a Life-Cycle Celebrant® with certification in Weddings. He lives on a beautiful lake in northern New Jersey with his husband and their two cocker spaniels. Jeff can be reached by email at jwalliscelebrant@aol.com.

The Labyrinth as Ceremonial Space

CHARLOTTE EULETTE

*"And in the end, the love you take
is equal to the love you make."*

– The Beatles

Giving gifts is something that we humans do. Usually, the gifts we give are tangible: they are presented in a wrapped box or festooned with a ribbon. But the gift of love is typically intangible…though often much more lasting.

There are times when I feel stumped trying to figure out what I can do or say to someone dear to me who is suffering and in need. Obviously, simply handing them a beautifully wrapped gift just won't do.

My friend Laura had just gone through her divorce. Her final decree papers came and she was relieved, but at the same time felt sad. I dashed over to her home and fetched her. We went to a garden in our town that has a labyrinth and we walked through together, at first in silence. We held hands for part of the circular trek. We laughed, cried, and tripped over each other. Once she smiled, I knew immediately that our labyrinth walk had done its magic! It's been seven years now since our first walk, but we still meet to ramble along the spiral path, thoughtfully tuning in and paying tribute to the miles of trials, tribulations, and triumphs in our lives.

Little did we know at the time that we had created our friendship's ceremonial space, something that needs no satin ribbon! Our walks are a timeless, healing, and beautiful gift that keeps on giving.

I invite you to try walking your own labyrinth! A labyrinth is a walking path, generally laid out in a circular design. Labyrinths have been used by people for eons as a meditative and contemplative tool. Celebrants use labyrinths for ritual and ceremony. Walking labyrinths can be found in parks or places of worship. However, you can make your own labyrinth from things you find in nature, such as sticks, sand, shells, or rocks.

PREPARATION

- Find a local labyrinth, or create your own winding labyrinth pathway in a park, wooded area, or field.

- Step into the labyrinth with an opened mind and heart.

- With every step, experience the rhythm of your walk like a heart beating.

- With every step, breathe in what you need and breathe out what you are letting go.

- Be present!

IN CLOSING

The labyrinth is your friend. Come back and visit soon. Bring others, too. Build it and they will come.

CHARLOTTE EULETTE is the International Director of the Celebrant Foundation & Institute and a Certified Life-Cycle Celebrant®. Charlotte lives in the great state of New Jersey with her family. She can be reached by email at charlotteeulette@celebrantinstitute.org.

When We Enter Silence

KEVIN O'BRIEN

Whenever I walked into the chapel at Christ's Peace House of Prayer in Easton, Kansas, I removed my shoes. The altar, which rested on dirt, was made of wood from the horse barn that once stood on that very spot. Beyond it was nothing but glass and a view of the forest.

Guests were invited to write their intentions into a prayer book on the altar. Incense was lit and Tibetan tingshas were struck three times. After introductory prayers, we entered ten minutes of silence rounded on both sides by a Japanese rin gong. Readings from a sacred text would follow, then intercessory prayers. A closing prayer and then the tingshas were struck three times: *peace*.

Returning home to Canton, Ohio, I greatly missed this daily ritual. And so I adapted it for use in everyday Life.

MATERIALS

Include something like the rin gong to focus the mind, something like incense to soothe the senses, an object to represent service or action, something with which to record your intentions, and an icon or image of inspiration.

PREPARATION

Begin with the ringing of a gong, the playing of a note, or the saying of special words.

ENTERING SILENCE

After the gong sounds, the ritual begins. To create the optimum flow of separation, transition, and reincorporation, I recommend you include the following elements:

- Opening prayers or meditation

- Silence

- Wisdom literature

- Intercessions or intentions for peace, healing, help, and thanksgiving

- A closing prayer or meditation

IN CLOSING

End with the sound you began with. Bow or bend your head profoundly and end with a word such as *Namaste*, which means, "I honor the light, the truth, the peace within you." Now you've set the tone for the day and created a place for eternal return.

KEVIN O'BRIEN is a Life-Cycle Celebrant® with certification in Funerals. He lives in North Canton, Ohio. He can be reached by email at kevinobrienceremonies@gmail.com or through his website, www.kevinobrienceremonies.com.

"THE EARTH HAS music FOR THOSE WHO listen"

—attributed to George Santayana

CHAPTER 2
Honoring the Elements

"We are made of star stuff," said the popular astronomer Carl Sagan. Sagan was echoing the words of the Harvard astronomer Harlow Shapley, who in 1929 was expanding upon a speech made in 1918 by the President of the Royal Astronomical Society in Canada. In the decades that followed, many other scientists and philosophers weighed in as well. Perhaps Shapley put it best:

> We are made of the same stuff as the stars. . . . Our very bodies consist of the same chemical elements found in the most distant nebulae, and our activities are guided by the same universal rules.

Some of these "universal rules" are only now becoming clear to us. Biologists have discovered, for example, that humans, other animals, and even plants experience circadian rhythms suggesting when to be active and when to rest. Circadian rhythms last about 24 hours, the same length of time as an Earth day. But we are ruled by other rhythms, too. Lunar rhythms influence our fertility. Seasonal rhythms encourage sowing, tending, reaping, and resting. And the rhythms we establish through our daily habits become enshrined in sense memory and also become part of who we are.

The ceremonies in this chapter are designed to help us dip into universal rhythms and remember that we are part of them. Cynthia Reed yokes the turning of the year to personal renewal. Lissin Lev Chaya suggests ways to honor the close of each day. Marguerite Griffin takes up the challenge of embracing change. Nikiah Seeds gets us in tune with the moon, and Sarah Lemp helps us celebrate the sun. Wendy Macdonald, Shevaun Rafferty, Rani Findlay, Woody Winfree, and I offer ways to celebrate trees, water, and pure sound.

An Annual Heroic Journey

CYNTHIA REED

When the calendar turns from December to January, or from one Chinese New Year to the next, or from one anniversary to the next, consider this thought: What if we treated each year of life as a hero's journey, a time for mindful renewal, a rite of passage? In all cultures and all times, the hero's journey is the archetypal rite of passage, showing the wanderings of a person in transformation who, after a series of ordeals and trials, finally returns to share his or her knowledge and be woven back into the fabric of society with a new status. What if we treated each new year as a new heroic journey, packed with potential for true change and wisdom?

MATERIALS

- An object to represent what you want to release and leave behind

- An object to represent something from the past that you want to bring forward

- An object to represent something you hope to discover

PREPARATION

Before you take that exhilarating but formidable first step, pause on the threshold to consciously mark the moment.

THE CEREMONY

- Release the first object to someone who can use it now that its useful life with you is complete.

- Take the second and third objects with you on a walk to a favorite outdoor place.

- Create a threshold using branches or stones, or simply draw a line on the ground.

- Hold the object representing last year in your hands and place the object representing your hopes for the year on the far side of your threshold.

- Meditate while standing on the threshold and, when you feel ready, cross it and pick up your object representing next year.

- When you return home, place your two objects on your dresser, desk, or altar, or take a photo of them to use as a screensaver.

IN CLOSING

Revisit your objects and journal once a month during the year as a touchstone. Crossing the threshold can be both frightening and thrilling, but remember: though the road ahead is unknown, its potential is rich!

CYNTHIA REED is a Master Life-Cycle Celebrant® with certification in Weddings, Funerals, Ceremonies Across the Life Cycle, and Ceremonies for Healing. She lives in the beautiful Blue Ridge Mountains in Asheville, North Carolina, with husband, daughters, and three dogs. Cindy can be reached by email at cynthiakreed@gmail.com.

Turning to the Next Morning

LISSIN LEV CHAYA

Ever since I was little, no matter where I was, I knew when the sun was going down. When I moved to the Pacific Coast fifteen years ago, my awareness prompted a daily sunset ritual. From the moment the bottom edge of the fireball hit the horizon until the moment it disappeared, my partner and I would sit in silence, simply watching. Often I was filled with gratitude at getting to witness the passage of another day. Now that I have a five-year-old in the house, silent sunsets are rare. Yet our sunset rituals live on.

PREPARATION

Find a comfortable place from which to witness the sunset.

TURNING TO THE NEXT MORNING

A Meditation for Adults: Go to the place you have found for viewing sunsets. Breathe. Offer general or specific gratitude for your day. Watch the sun sink—in silence, if possible—from the moment it hits your horizon until it is gone. Take another breath to set your experience in ritual.

The Children's Ritual: Children often prefer movement, action, and sound to silence. These days, my partner and I sit together with my son and any other kids who are around at sunset, and we sing:

> Goodnight to the Sun for another day
>
> Thanks for the light, thanks for the play.
>
> Now we'll watch you slip away,
>
> And we'll see you again tomorrow.

IN CLOSING

Taking time to honor the passage of the day can reopen our lives to the subtleties of nature and bring us deeper into connection with the whole. Acknowledging the sunset and the rhythm of the day can help bring us into awareness of the now and strengthen our ability to be present to the rest of our lives.

LISSIN LEV CHAYA is a Life-Cycle Celebrant® with certification in Weddings. She lives in a magical cove on the Pacific Ocean just down the beach from San Francisco with her beloved and her young son. Lissin can be reached by email at celebrant@lissinsong.com or through her website, www.lissinsong.com.

A Celtic Imbolc Celebration

PATRICIA EAGLE

Midwinter is a transition point, a time for reflecting on the last year and planning the next one. The Celtic mid-winter celebration called Imbolc offers a way to navigate the rhythms of death and rebirth, decay and renewal. It's a way to celebrate the dark and light that happen all around and inside of us. It's also viewed as a time to celebrate the lives of all those who have taught and prepared us and nurtured the soil of our souls.

PREPARATION
Begin with an invocation or responsive reading. Or sing!

THE CEREMONY
- Honor those who have nurtured us and scatter their names like seeds. Take a moment to think of those who have gone to the heart of what matters to you. Now say their names out loud, scattering them like seeds in the soil of Mother Earth.

- Consider soil and seeds. Think of it: in reality we are both soil and seed. We all nurture one another's growth, and we look for safe and healthy places of our own in which to root and grow. Honor this reality by planting seeds or starter herbs.

- Consider the cycles of dark and light. Use light and darkness in meditation to sync yourself with the cycles of the seasons:

  — Imagine yourself a seed, deep in the arms of earth. The earth is hard and heavy, but you can sense the light above you.

  — Imagine yourself slowly pushing upward toward the air. It's difficult, as life often is, but you know you can make it.

— Visualize yourself breaking through the soil. Stretch up toward the sky with confidence, feeling your firm roots in the earth.

— Imagine your new life being called to emerge. See your infant hopes and dreams being gently coaxed into reality.

IN CLOSING

Write out and decorate these classic pondering questions for the season of Imbolc:

• How is beauty seeking to express itself in your life?

• What is being initiated in your life at this time?

• What do you most need, and what help is at hand?

PATRICIA EAGLE is a Life-Cycle Celebrant® with certification in Weddings and Funerals. Patricia lives in the vast and beautiful San Luis Valley in Alamosa, Colorado, with her beloved spouse and two very ornery but sweet dogs. She can be reached by email at horizonsceremonies@gmail.com or through her website, www.horizonsceremonies.com.

Embrace the Equinox

MARGUERITE H. GRIFFIN

On or about March 21 each year, daylight and darkness are nearly equal in all parts of the world. In the northern hemisphere, we embrace the vernal equinox as the beginning of spring. It's is the time for spring cleaning and for letting go of the old and embracing the new. As temperatures gradually rise and spirits become buoyant, we recommit to New Year's resolutions made in the darkness of winter and imagine moving forward to a brighter future.

PREPARATION

In ancient civilizations, clocks and calendars made use of the sun's light to mark the seasons for sowing seeds and harvesting crops. Today, we may reflect on the seeds that we've planted and the work we've done in the gardens of our relationships, our families, and our life's path. We can contemplate things lost and gained and consider how to make room for new growth.

- Examine those areas in your life where you may feel challenged, inert, or stuck.

- Consider first your external environment. Imagine how you'd like to make space for abundance, clarity, or simplicity.

- Consider your internal environment—your personal habits, practices, and proclivities. How are your dreams coming along? What would you like to have or create more of as spring progresses to summer?

BEGIN AGAIN!

Beginning again may be as simple as undertaking a new activity, one that will remind you of your commitment to growth. You might decide to keep a daily journal and review it at each full moon. Or you might want to take up a new hobby, assist with planting flower bulbs in a community garden, or participate in a meditation or yoga class.

IN CLOSING

Especially at transitional times, give yourself the gift of time. Include in that gift the permission to experience a new thing each day. You can top off your gift to yourself by listing those things for which you are already grateful. As you reconnect to the rhythm of your life, be open to sharing your experiences with others!

MARGUERITE H. GRIFFIN is a Life-Cycle Celebrant® with certification in Weddings. She lives in Chicago and can be reached by email at meaningfulmarguerite@gmail.com or through her website, www.meaningfulmarguerite.com

Gratitude Offering To Trees

RANI FINDLAY & WOODY WINFREE

This ceremony of collaborative service to trees took root in the Western desert, under the stewardship of an indigenous healer and global leader dedicated to the continuity of life on earth. Active expressions of gratitude are the seeds of healing and nourishment for Mother Earth. As the smallest stone initiates unending ripples in a pond, this powerful ceremony initiates a far-reaching vibration of gratitude and healing for all trees.

MATERIALS

- Bowl of water
- Ribbon

THE TREEBUTE

- Choose to honor a tree you've planted, a favorite tree you encounter, or even a plant that you enjoy.

- Stand before the tree, indoors or out, state your intention. Express your gratitude for all trees sustaining our life on Mother Earth.

- Enter sacred space. Breathe, hum, rattle, sing, ring a bell, or light a candle or incense.

- Offer a blessing. Hold a small bowl of water in your hands and recite words such as the following:

  Beloved tree, by your existence my life is sustained and nurtured. By your existence I live and love. I offer you my gratitude. May you be protected, nourished, healed, and sustained. May you—and all trees and all forests—be recognized and cherished.

- Pour the water that now carries your words of blessing onto the base of the tree.

IN CLOSING

- Connect to the tree by touching, embracing, and/or tying a ribbon around it, knowing that all trees receive your offering.

RANI FINDLAY is a Life-Cycle Celebrant® with certification in Weddings, Funerals, and Ceremonies Across the Life Cycle. She lives in western Massachusetts and can be reached through her website, www.ranithecelebrant.com.

WOODY WINFREE is a Life-Cycle Celebrant® with certification in Weddings and Funerals. She lives in north Florida and can be reached through her website, www.woodywinfree.com.

Inward with the New Moon

NIKIAH SEEDS

In the past month there was new moon in the sky. Did you notice it? That was a trick question. The new moon, or dark moon, is the time of the month when the moon rises as the sun rises and sets as the sun sets. We can't see the new moon because it's too close to the sun's glare to be visible. It's there, though—just as our goals and intentions remain even when we lose sight of them.

MATERIALS
- Favorite cozy spot
- Paper
- Pen or pencil

PREPARATION
The phase of the new moon is a good time for turning inward and a great time for new beginnings. Just as the moon goes inward for a few nights a month and then is reborn again to grow in the sky, we can also turn inward to reflect and then enter the next week feeling fresh and renewed.

INWARD WITH THE NEW MOON
Adopting the new moon as a magical time of new beginnings, take a few moments to enter into peace and recharge your intentions.

- Close your eyes and take a few mindful breaths.

- Consider goals you would like to set or re-enliven. Be gentle with yourself. Focus on finding inspiration for your goals.

- Once you feel ready, write down your goals with a focus on renewal and inspiration for the next month.

IN CLOSING

I like to think of the new moon as "the resting moon." Symbolically, the moon takes a rest from its duties in the night sky for a few days every month. When it returns, it's ready to blaze forth in the night sky.

NIKIAH SEEDS is a Life-Cycle Celebrant® with certification in Weddings. She lives in Vancouver, Canada, and can be reached by email at nikiahseeds@gmail.com or through her website, www.redmoonceremonies.com.

Living, Essential Water

WENDY MACDONALD

Water cleanses, purifies, restores, and heals. One has only to experience a blooming desert, a sprouting seed, a clean body, or the sense of well-being that follows a refreshing, hydrating drink to grasp its value. Humanity celebrates its spiritual connection to the sacred essence of water with washing and immersion rituals, baptisms, and prayer. Here is another way to make the celebration of water a conscious part of your day.

MATERIALS

Clean, fresh water

PREPARATION

Consciously release negative thoughts and feelings, letting go of the past and forgiving yourself and others.

HYDRATION APPRECIATION

When you're filling a bathtub or preparing to step into a shower, bring awareness to your actions and resolve to make conservation a ritual practice.

- As the water flows from its source to you, say, "Thank you water, blessed water." Feel the water cleanse your skin and energy field.

- Allow shower pressure and the warmth of the water to relax tense muscles and reach core places in your mind and heart. Visualize toxins, pain, and negative thoughts flowing with the water down the drain and say, "Thank you water, healing water."

- As you step refreshed into the flow of your day, remember how water supports life as flowers burst into bloom; insects, reptiles and birds dance and mate; and humans and mammals bathe, splash, and play. With exuberant gratitude, say, "Thank you water, precious water."

IN CLOSING

You can include this ritual in other moments, too. When watering a houseplant or a garden, when filling a dish with clean, fresh water for your pet, when preparing to drink from a water-filled glass or bottle, or before you step or dive into a natural body of water, say, "Thank you water, precious water," and grace the moment with a ritual act.

WENDY MACDONALD is a Life-Cycle Celebrant® with certification in Weddings and Funerals. She lives in New Hampshire within easy driving distance of Maine, New Jersey, and Vermont. Wendy can be reached by email at wendy.nhcelebrant@gmail.com or through her website, www.seasonsoftheheartne.rr.com.

Centering with Solstice Mandalas

SARAH LEMP

In the northern hemisphere, the summer solstice marks the first day of summer, the time when mother earth's plans come to fruition. This is a great time to build upon nature's riches and meditate on the outcomes you want to manifest in your life.

MATERIALS

- A quiet location in which to build your mandala

- Dried herbs and spices of your choice

- Notebook or journal

- Pen or pencil

- Yellow and orange flower petals of your choice

PREPARATION

- Gather or purchase yellow and orange flowers such as daisies, black-eyed susans, nasturtiums, sunflowers, mums, and marigolds. You can also use dried herbs or spices like turmeric, dried chili peppers, chamomile, safflowers, and calendula petals.

- Select a sunny, quiet spot where you will not be disturbed— preferably, somewhere outside.

THE MANDALA

Center yourself by taking a few deep breaths. Then make a mental list of the things you want to renew, manifest, enhance, or release from your life. You may want to recite some affirmations or mantras as you place each flower petal in place.

- Starting from the center, carefully arrange the flower petals in a circular pattern. Give yourself freedom from perfection. Allow the spontaneous "artist" to emerge.

- When you have finished building your mandala, use it as a focal point for a meditation ranging from ten minutes to a half hour or more. Take a few deep breaths and gaze into the center. Without judgment, notice your thoughts and feelings. What images come to mind? What feelings bubble up to the surface?

IN CLOSING

Creative expression can help you recall your higher purpose, and using objects that represent the season helps align your energy with nature's rhythms. When the winter solstice arrives, try making a winter mandala using pine needles, holly, juniper berries, star anise, cinnamon bark, allspice, dried oranges, and peppermint!

SARAH LEMP is a Life-Cycle Celebrant® with certification in Weddings. She and her musican husband, Chris, live with their gorgeous Himalayan in Southern California. Sarah can be reached by email at sarah@sarahmony.com or through her website, www.sarahmony.com.

The Great Symphony of Life

SHEVAUN RAFFERTY

Modern techniques of brain imaging have shown that sound can have a notable impact on the brain's endorphin centers. And experience tells us that we are touched by music and sounds in more ways than we may ever consciously know. Be alive to the impact of sound in your life!

MATERIALS

Required: Your own ears
Optional: a bell, a Tibetan bowl, or your own voice

ONE-STEP WAYS TO PLAY IN THE GREAT SYMPHONY OF LIFE

- Connect with the natural world around you by listening to raindrops splattering, insects buzzing, the wind whistling around skyscrapers, or the breath of a loved one.

- Take time to listen to another human being with full and unbiased attention. You will hear more than you heard before. You may find that you both have reopened your hearts and renewed your spirits.

- Lift your spirits and open your heart. Listen to live local music or recorded music without doing anything else at the same time.

- Visit a church with a choir and join in. Or make your own music. Not so long ago people whistled or hummed as they worked, mothers sang to their kids, and hymns were not just for the choir. When you sing or make music, both creating and hearing sound waves, you open your heart twice.

- Ring a Tibetan bowl or sound a bell. Listen to the reverberations as they gently fade. You will find your head has been cleared, and for a moment you will hear silence—the sound of the universe before it takes its next noisy breath.

IN CLOSING

Music and musical sounds can be a great way to bring our minds, hearts, and spirits into the very vibration they need to be whole. Surround yourself with sound—choose wisely—and you will find yourself opened and renewed.

SHEVAUN RAFFERTY is a Life-Cycle Celebrant® with certification in Weddings, Funerals, and Ceremonies Across the Life Cycle. She lives on the north coast of Northern Ireland with her husband and the two youngest of her six children. She can be reached by email at shevaunr@gmail.com or through her website, www.seasons-of-light.org.

Poet-Trees

SHERI REDA

Nature, they say, abhors a vacuum—which may be why we fill the space between us with communications of all kinds. During busy times, we email, post, text, and tweet and are surprised when we look up and see a flesh-and-blood face. Poetry posts are a way to combine human connection and a connection with nature. They are like those real estate signs that hold listing sheets, except that instead of listings, they hold and display poems, quotes, or words of wisdom. They range in complexity from imitation trail markers to unprotected pages attached to trees, which turns trees into—yes—poet-trees.

MATERIALS

- Materials for posting, such as a length of string or a pre–built box

- Statement, wish, quote, or poem honoring nature

- Tree or lamppost

- Unbleached paper

PREPARATION

Find a quote or poem that honors nature and may inspire human beings. Print it out or copy it by hand and live with it for a week to make sure it speaks to you in a variety of moods. Then consider the kind of experience you want to offer.

- Do you want to post a single page that people come to see, or a product people can take with them? Will your posting be ephemeral—designed to wear away over time—or encased in a permanent or semi-permanent home?

- Be sure that laws or regulations permit you to post materials in your chosen spot. Your own parkway or lawn may be the best spot for a posting; city and parkland kiosks can work, too.

THE POST

Set an intention, post your material, then become the first reader to read the post aloud. Let the sound steep the area with good intentions.

THE CLOSING

Ceremonies and rituals are all about making words and intentions come alive. By posting them to share with friends and strangers alike, you invite ceremony and an appreciation for nature into everyone's life, and you contribute to a truly social form of media.

SHERI REDA is a Mster Life-Cycle Celebrant® with certification in Weddings, Funerals, Ceremonies Across the Life Cycle, and Ceremonies for Healing. She lives in Chicago with her husband and the younger of her two great kids. Sheri can be reached by email at sheri.a.reda@gmail.com or through her website, www.flowceremonies.com.

"love,
I FIND, IS LIKE
singing"

— Zora Neale Hurston

CHAPTER 3

Connecting With Self & Others

Next time you find yourself at a tourist attraction, a suburban mall, or even a very large department store, stop for a moment and treat yourself to the spiritual direction at your fingertips. It's right there, on the map of the place—an X symbol, and the magic words:

YOU ARE HERE.

The trick is in remembering the miracle of existence, even while enjoying (or surviving) the cacophony of ordinary life. The ceremonies in this chapter help us do just that.

Some of these ceremonies are all about the part of us that sits quietly and reaches inward, nurturing inner peace to have something to share. Tulis McCall invites us to welcome new perspectives regarding our tenancy here on the "fragile blue marble" of Earth. Diane Wilkerson suggests ways to be kind to your telecommuting peer group of one. Cristina Kollet highlights opportunities for "moments of mindfulness" in an ordinary day. ChrisTina Simek's way of the jester reminds us "Life's too mysterious—don't take it serious!" And Beth Palubinsky shows that when serious happens, we can honor it with mindfulness and compassion.

Other ceremonies celebrate our interconnectedness. Alethea Devi promotes the establishment of an Interdependence Day. Jessie Blum offers one-step commitment ceremonies to support relationships and personal goals. Holly Pruett reveals ways to do self-reflection among friends. Caroline Flanders embraces the larger community, offering rites to honor everyone whose sacrifices serve the greater good. Kristine Bentz suggests eco-friendly valentine rites, proving that we can love ourselves, our friends, and our lovely Mother Earth all at once!

Reaching for the Moon (Again)

TULIS MCCALL

After July 20, 1969, when human beings first set foot on the moon, we never looked up at her again in quite the same way. Our journey to the moon also changed the way we looked at Earth. This first human sighting of Earth—the "fragile blue marble" surrounded by black space—changed our understanding of the planet from something invincible to something fragile that needs our attention, commitment, and care. What elements of your life might benefit from the same kind of change in perspective?

MATERIALS

- Paper
- Pen or pencil

RITUAL FOR CHANGING PERSPECTIVE

- Lie on the ground, on the floor, or on a bed or couch. Slowly look up and from side to side. Take special note of two or three objects or locations you can see.

- Sit up and look around slowly. Note what you can see that was previously out of sight. Gaze at the objects or areas you previously noted. How are they different?

- Stand up and slowly look around. Once again, examine those objects or locations you chose. What is different now? What were you sitting on that you could not see before?

- Rise up on your toes three times. As you lift yourself, notice the change in your perspective. It is small but mighty.

- Finally, write down three areas of your life where you feel stuck.

Closet need clearing out? Client pool shrinking? Relationship not going so well? Write it down.

- Then flip your statements. Instead of saying "My closet needs cleaning out," try "I need cleaning out." Instead of, "I need more clients," try "More clients need me." Instead of "My partner is getting on my nerves," try "I might be getting on my partner's nerves." Write down these new perspectives. Say them out loud. How do they feel and how do you feel saying them?

IN CLOSING

With every moonrise, there is an earthrise. When you bring a new perspective to a problem, there is a shift. With that shift comes new possibilities. We just need to change our perspective in order to see them, just as we did when we stepped upon the moon.

TULIS MCCALL is a Life-Cycle Celebrant® certified in Weddings. She lives and works throughout the New York Metro Area. You can reach Tulis through her websites, www.weddingsbytulis.com or at www.newyorkweddingofficiant.org.

Interdependence Days

ALETHEA DEVI

Each summer, communities throughout The United States and Canada celebrate their independence. To be part of a community, however, is also to acknowledge and even celebrate your interdependence. One way to do that is to offer a blessing ritual in recognition of valued members of the community.

MATERIALS

Required: Invitations to a combination party and blessing ritual

Optional: Wand or feather for directing the blessing process

PREPARATION

Create a framework like a woven basket, with both structure and openness. Suggest time or content limits, but let magic happen!

PERFORMING MAGIC

- Place the celebrated person in the center of your circle. Invite guests to arrange themselves loosely around him or her.

- Gently touch or tap the forehead, hands, heart area, and perhaps feet of the honoree, offering blessings or good wishes in word such as, "May you always walk in beauty."

- One at a time, invite each individual guest to give voice to the unspoken ways in which he or she appreciates the honoree. Amazing words and gestures will flow forth. Honor them all, summarize and echo them as you end the ceremony with words of love.

IN CLOSING

Remember the gifts of solemnity as well as humor, because life is full of both. Good luck, and may the magic of interdependence cloak and comfort you!

ALETHEA DEVI is a Life-Cycle Celebrant® with certification in Weddings and Funerals. She lives just a short walk from the Willamette River in Portland, Oregon, with her musician husband, Dennis, and their big black cat. Alethea can be reached by email at aletheadevi@gmail.com or through her website, www.aletheadeviceremonies.com.

For Those Who Work Alone

DIANE WILKERSON

Almost every day, as you drive, bike, or walk to work, you encounter people along the way. You greet a bus driver, barista, guards at the door, and perhaps receptionist on your way to your space. If you're a regular, you may enjoy a hearty greeting and a smile or two along the way. You meet and greet co-workers at the water cooler, coffeepot, or rest room and engage in light conversation, perhaps collecting more smiles. Perhaps this is a team-building day, with a group meeting, picnic, or some other outing that allows you to relax a bit, have a few laughs, and interact in a casual fashion.

Unless you are a teleworker. By choice or by chance, increasingly greater numbers of people now work from a home office. There are upsides, of course. No gas-wasting commute! Your own coffee! Meetings in your pajamas (if you aren't on Skype)! All these benefits make for an easier day in many respects.

Still, telecommuters pay for their perks through their lack of personal connections with other actual humans. Most telecommuter "meetings" take place via telephone, most correspondence comes through e-mail. No one is waiting to hang out with you over coffee (except for your cat, who doesn't want to talk to you anyway!).

As a telecommuter, you probably don't get that external affirmation that comes from being part of a larger group. What to do? Connect with yourself. Create your own daily "commuting" rituals.

CONNECTING

- Welcome yourself into your workday. Take a moment to look at yourself in the mirror. Give yourself a BIG SMILE and say, "Hello! Let's have a great day."

- During your lunch hour (OK, lunch minute), take time for some refreshing deep-breathing exercises.

- At the end of your day, no matter what kind of day you've had, go back to that mirror with a smile and say, "Thank you."

IN CLOSING

Receiving your affirmations and gratitude makes for a much nicer "commute." And remember, all of the above works well for conventional commuters too!

DIANE WILKERSON is Life-Cycle Celebrant® with certification in Weddings and Funerals. She and her rose garden live in Monmouth County, New Jersey. Diane can be reached at dvw2010@aol.com.

Renewing Your Commitments

JESSIE BLUM

When we think about renewing commitments, many people think of a second wedding—a public ceremony followed by a reception. But commitments take many forms, and renewals can, too.

In a relationship, renewal can be a private affair. You can share an activity you both enjoy (a nice dinner out, a relaxing walk, or even a movie you can watch together at home), and afterward, take a moment to recommit yourselves to your relationship.

In your own life, take a moment to remember those New Year's resolutions you made back in January. How are you doing on them? If you haven't been successful, consider taking the opportunity to recommit yourself to these goals.

ONE-STEP RENEWAL CEREMONIES

- Romance Renewal. A simple and easy sharing ritual is to remove your wedding bands and hand them to each other, each partner taking a moment to hold and warm the ring in their hands, infusing it with love. Then, with awareness, place the ring back onto your partner's finger. Take a sweet moment to reflect on what is important and to make sure your partner knows how much he or she is appreciated.

- Goal Renewal. Once you have decided upon a new commitment or goal, find an object that represents that goal to you, whether it's something like a whole piece of fresh fruit for eating better or a pencil for taking more time to write. Set your intention by lighting a candle, and then envision yourself completing or working toward your goal every day. Place the symbolic object in a prominent place in your home, someplace where you will see it everyday, and let it act as a reminder to continue practicing your new habit.

IN CLOSING

To strengthen your ties to your loved ones, your goals, and yourself, ask yourself, *What commitments can I renew?*

JESSIE BLUM is a Life-Cycle Celebrant® with certification in Weddings and Ceremonies Across the Life Cycle. Jessie lives in Bergen County, New Jersey, with her husband and two cats. She can be reached through her website, www.eclectic-unions.com.

Sustenance Rituals to Replenish the Well

CRISTINA KOLLET

If you're like me, mid-January is the season of the post-holiday crash. During the winter holiday season rituals abound, but afterward I'm faced with a dry well. Once a holiday or great event is over, how do we refill that ritual well? How do we return refreshed to our lives, to new plans and older plans already underway?

ONE-STEP MOMENTS OF MINDFULNESS

Sustenance rituals are little moments of mindfulness we can use to catch our breath and find our center. I think of them as elements of personal maintenance, ways to take care of and reconnect with ourselves. Here are a few easy ones you can work into your daily routine:

- Take the stairs. You can make a walking meditation out of taking the stairs. This can be especially helpful at the end of your workday. Feel the rhythm of each step you take. With each step, leave behind some of the troubles of your day and think about getting closer to the comforts of home or some activity you're looking forward to. By the time you have reached the bottom step, you may feel a little less burdened—and ready to reenter the world.

- Get some light. Many of us suffer from the winter blues, and if you work long hours, odds are that you don't ever get as much sunlight as you would like. So make some time to step outside. Take a walk during your lunch break or look out the window. It's an easy way to literally brighten your day.j58

- Sort it out. The simple act of sorting can be a way to bring symbolic order to chaos. So sort your socks. Or dump your change jar and sort the coins. I sometimes sort a mason jar of buttons as a tool for mindfulness. Putting things in their place can be very calming.

IN CLOSING

These all may seem like simple things. Perhaps some of them are things you already do. What makes it a sustenance ritual, though, is mindful action. Set a clear intention when you do these things, and then do them with purpose to take care of yourself. That will make these everyday actions that much more potent.

CRISTINA KOLLET is a Master Life-Cycle Celebrant® with certification in Weddings, Funerals, and Ceremonies Across the Life Cycle. She lives in New Jersey with her husband, Paul, and their pride of cats. Cristina can be reached by email at cris@inclusiveceremonies.com or through her website, www.inclusiveceremonies.com.

Holding Up the Mirror

HOLLY PRUETT

A young woman I once worked with, a star in her 20s, entered a painful crisis of confidence in her 30s—what Joseph Campbell would call "The Road of Trials." She chose to embrace this journey with the following ceremony, which encourages self-reflection and fosters self-confidence.

MATERIALS
- Basket
- Words of comfort or support

PREPARATION
For this kind of ceremony, you need to bring together a set of people you trust. The group will become a mirror in which you see yourself reflected back as the brave and precious person you are.

HOLDING UP THE MIRROR
- Set your intention for the ceremony, including a few words of thanks for the people who have come together as a group to support you.

- Ask each participant in your ceremony to choose a word from a basket. The words should represent positive qualities such as patience, resilience, and fearlessness.

- As each person shares the word he or she has selected, that person must embody the word for the group. Curiosity may become a wondering look around; community becomes an embrace. Enacted around the circle, the words became a potent dance, reminding you that you have everything you need within yourself.

IN CLOSING

Whenever you need a boost, invite your allies to share what they see in you. They can join you in person or contribute long-distance to rituals or even moments of support. Remember, you can call on your community to hold up a mirror when your reflection becomes clouded!

HOLLY PRUETT is a Life-Cycle Celebrant® with certification in Funerals and Ceremonies Across the Life Cycle. She lives in Portland, Oregon, with her life partner, Amber, and their two cats. Holly can be reached by email at holly@hollypruettcelebrant.com or through her website, www.hollypruettcelebrant.com.

Honoring Those Who Serve

CAROLINE FLANDERS

In 1962, President John F. Kennedy established Armed Forces Day as an official holiday to honor personnel in all branches of the military, including the Army, Navy, Marine Corps, Air Force, and Coast Guard. In these troubled times, we can widen our observance to show appreciation for all individuals who act upon their personal conviction of selfless service in the way they see fit.

PREPARATION

Consider personal sacrifices and separations people have endured and still endure in the name of patriotism, valor, or service to others. Remember those of your own family or generation or cohort who have volunteered and proudly served their community or their nation.

ONE-STEP RITES FOR HONORING OTHERS

- Throughout the country, parades and celebrations are scheduled in remembrance of military personnel, laborers, and others. Consider joining in one of these events. Be present to the personal pride and the emotions on display. Open up to individual stories behind the faces of the men and women who stand ready to serve the country. What are some of the ways you can recognize and show appreciation for military personnel and others as a catalyst for peace in the world?

- Take a moment of your day during Armed Forces Week, Veterans Day, Labor Day, or another holiday to reflect on the lives of your own ancestors. How did their actions shape your life today? How did their participation and devotion to their ideals influence you? How do you participate in a tradition of service to your community or country?

IN CLOSING

Open your mind, be present, and embrace your emotions and feelings about service. With critical thinking, choose to recognize lives of purpose and personal meaning. Celebrate those who stand in integrity, being authentic to their personal higher calling.

CAROLINE FLANDERS is a Life-Cycle Celebrant® certified in Funerals. She lives and works in Southern California. Caroline can be reached by email at caroline@celebrantoflife.com.

Bound, Unbound, Boundless

CHRISTINA SIMEK

Welcome to the Jesting School, an altered realm of creativity, openness, and awareness, where play-filled "being-ness" exists unbound. There are no judgments here, nor boundaries, nor rules. You will be held irresponsible to sign an unbinding contract—sign here, on the undaunted line. If you are willing, please step forward and enter the land of unconditional acceptance.

NO PREPARATION NECESSARY!

ONE-STEP JESTING

- The Joker Is Wild. Carelessly choose a piece of wild music. Feel the rhythms; let them move you. Now get up and flail around. Dance wildly! Let go and experience the jest from head to toe.

- Orientation of the Fool. Step outside yourself, literally. Take a walk in nature (or, if you' re deep inside a city, simply stand in front of a tree). Let yourself become quiet inside nature's embrace. Hear the songbirds sing, feel the sun's warmth, let it all touch you. Now, just be. Let your true inner nature shine through.

- Fools School 102. Learn from the Masters of Play. Spend time with a child and let the child guide you. Get down on your hands and knees and see what the child sees. Give in to a sense of joy and wonderment, the purity of a child at play.

- Answer the Knock. When opportunity comes, leap into action — shape-shift your space for coming attractions. Add a bit of color. Create a new space. Go at your personal jester's pace.

IN CLOSING

As jesters and jokers you must wear your goals or your cape or your emotions proudly. Dance and laugh and express yourself loudly. Fellow jesters, here is the key to the kingdom — the unbound, boundless new happiness: freedom.

CHRISTINA SIMEK is a Life-Cycle Celebrant® with certification in Funerals and Weddings. She lives in beautiful and inspiring Santa Fe, New Mexico. Christina can be reached by email at christina@heartscrossing.com.

Eco-Friendly Valentines

KRISTINE BENTZ

In the years since their nineteenth-century origins, simple and loving Valentine's traditions have given way to a commercialized hustle of candy, roses, and singing cards. But handcrafted gifts still lend a special air to Valentine's Day—and any other day!

PREPARATION

First, focus less on commercially driven gifting. Instead, look for more spirited and environmentally friendly exchanges between sweethearts, friends, family, and even animal companions. Second, open up your great imagination to the flow of creative juices.

A MENU OF ONE-STEP VALENTINE RITES

Here are a few ideas for infusing Valentine's Day with friendly spirit and eco-friendly creativity this year.

- Write a poem to someone beloved and embellish it with symbolic items or drawings. Show love for Earth as well by placing your poem on handcrafted recycled or natural materials.

- Gather friends for an evening of home-cooked foods and storytelling about love gained, sustained, or lost.

- Create homemade biscuits for animal companions. Share them with canine companions at the dog park, equine buddies at the stable, or feline fans in your building.

- Have a collage party to celebrate love. Ask invitees to gather objects of meaning that represent all the aspects of love. These may be found in a jewelry box, in nature, in storage, or at the thrift store. Guests may also bring their own picture frames, small altars, clay pots, memento boxes, and other objects and use collage to decorate them.

IN CLOSING

Bring your own spin to any of these ideas. Or just celebrate your friends and loved ones with less superfluous fluff and more heartfelt care. Be surprised—and enjoy!

KRISTINE BENTZ is a Life-Cycle Celebrant® with certification in Weddings, Funerals, and Ceremonies for Healing. She lives in the Sonoran Desert with her life partner and their animal companions, an opinionated white mare and two kittens. Kristine can be reached through her website, www.sweetgrassceremonies.com.

In Times of Trouble

BETH PALUBINSKY

More than a dozen outstanding Japanese ball players were at
Major League Baseball's spring training in 2011 when news rushed
at us unrelentingly from Japan that an almost unfathomably
devastating earthquake and tsunami had hit the coast.

PREPARATION

Consider the words of second baseman Tsuyoshi Nishioka, who had
arrived only recently at the ballpark in Ft. Myers, Florida, to start his
first season with the Minnesota Twins. Asked if he'd thought about
sitting out the game—after all, spring training games don't count,
really—he said,

> That came across my mind at first, but since I am here,
> challenging the United States as a Japanese person, I
> understand that I am in an occupation where I can relay
> dreams and hope and energy back to Japan. I wanted to
> be on the field and think about people back home and
> give my all out on the field, to give some of that back.

Nishioka went 1 for 2 with a walk, and the Twins took the game 3-2
from the Red Sox.

USING RITUAL TO HELP

We can and should celebrate all our seasons, staying deeply mindful
of what's happening in other places across the planet. Honor and
practice your spring rituals, whether breaking out your team tie,
cramming the first spring pansies into flower boxes, raking up winter's
brown cover of yard leaves, or decorating eggs for Easter baskets.

Light a candle before you begin, taking a moment to watch the light shimmer and the delicate smoke rise into the air. Imagine your good wishes riding on those wisps of light and smoke. Then carry your hopes and dreams into the world, as Tsuyohi Nishioka did each time he took to the field.

IN CLOSING

No matter where you are or what your abilities, you can connect the special and the mundane, the calm of your world with the chaos of someone else's. You share common ground with every human being, and your ritual acts just might send some inspiration their way.

BETH PALUBINSKY is a Life-Cycle Celebrant® with certification in Funerals, Ceremonies Across the Life Cycle, and Ceremonies for Healing. She and her husband live in Philadelphia, a short trolley ride from the heart of the city. Beth can be reached by email at bethcelebrant@gmail.com.

"BEING DEEPLY
loved
BY SOMEONE GIVES YOU
strength...
LOVING SOMEONE DEEPLY GIVES YOU
courage"

—Lao Tzu

CHAPTER 4

Roots & Wings

What is a family? The etymology of the word reveals that ancient Roman family members thought of themselves as "servants of the household."

For most of history, families have been large, interrelated groups of grandparents, parents, and children living under the same roof. In the Victorian era the definition shrank, and people came to think of family as a group of parents and children living together. We call it the nuclear family. But the "nuclear option" is far from the only way to go. There are many ways to surround yourself with supportive, committed loved ones. Families today include close and distant relatives, adopted members, and "families of choice." They are created out of commitment and love, and they include the ancestors who have lit our way. All these are something to celebrate.

In this chapter, Marilyn Rampley reminds us of the ritual value of family stories and traditions such as storytime. She highlights the link they create between generations. Kim Nash suggests a variety of ways to honor and thank our ancestors, and Ivy Cox shines a spotlight on a particular ceremony adopted with respect from Taiwan. Lest we forget our living, breathing elders, Diane Gansauer outlines a tribute ceremony you can construct with the help of the very person you want to honor.

There's more. Lois Heckman advocates widespread use of sand ceremonies to support the blending of newly forming families. Dana Zipkin unearths opportunities for ceremony within the everyday rituals that make up family life. Cindy Matchett gifts us with a multitude of tips for keeping all your ceremonies family-friendly, and Annemarie Juhlian reminds us that pets are part of the family, too.

Each of these ceremonies is specific, and yet each can be adopted to fit any group you live with or love. A family is no longer defined by parents and children or even by household. But it's still a great container for belonging and a worthy thing to serve!

"Tell Us a Story!"

MARILYN RAMPLEY

Once when we were away from home with no books available, I told my grandchildren a story about when their parents were little. From that moment on, a new tradition reigned. And as my grandchildren grow, my treasure chest of remembered stories has grown into a very large trunk.

PREPARATION

First we do all the prep needed to go to bed—baths, teeth, meds, etc. Then we turn out the lights and get comfortable. Next they make requests, which rotate between calling up favorite, formerly-shared stories and asking for brand new ones. Every time I think I can't possibly remember yet another story, some hint from the grandkids prompts a new one.

THE STORIES

Coming up with stories can be brain-taxing, but the stories are there, in categories ranging from specific to general. Specifics might include the time Grandpa Ray got sprayed by a skunk, the time you got lost and there was lightning, or the time firefighters came to the block. General categories range from a story about Mom that we've never heard before to a funny one about Dad that happened at school. You can also share a story about a time when you were sad, scared, or worried.

IN CLOSING

Recently I attended a volunteer luncheon highlighting this quote from Robert McKee: "Stories are the creative conversion of life itself into a more powerful, clearer, more meaningful experience. They are the currency of human contact."

Bedtime stories are profound sharing tools for a collectively remembered past with affirmations about who we are as a family, what our place is in the world, and what we consider important. They wrap our past, present, and future together into one pleasurable, meaningful bundle.

Marilyn Rampley is a Life-Cycle Celebrant® with certification in Funerals and Ceremonies Across the Life Cycle. She and her husband, Greg, live close to their six grandchildren in Phoenix, Arizona. Marilyn can be reached by email at rampleyaz@msn.com or through her website, www.life-cyclecelebrations.com.

Closer Than We Think

KIM NASH

Many of us are descendants of people who made sacrifices so that we could live "a better life." We owe it to them and to ourselves as heirs to think about our history, learn about our ancestors, and honor some of their traditions in our own lives.

MATERIALS

Variable, depending on your vision

DOING THE HONORS

The following are some one-step ways to keep memories of ancestors alive and to share your own heritage with others, especially children.

- Display a photograph. Take your old family photos out of storage and place them in frames around your home. Learn about the people in the photographs and share your discoveries with anyone who asks.

- Use your family heirlooms. If you've acquired a set of china, a tablecloth, silverware, or a family recipe . . . use it! On holidays or other special occasions, incorporate some these heritage items into your own traditions.

- Visit a special memorial site. Many commemorative places honor our ancestors. Take a trip to visit one. If your ancestor's name is etched on the Wall of Honor at Ellis Island, or if they have a gravestone, take a rubbing. Keep it among other heirloom treasures.

IN CLOSING

There is no better way to honor our ancestors than by bringing them close and keeping their memory alive. Along the way, you may discover that they really are closer to you than ever you could have imagined.

Kim S. Nash is a Life-Cycle Celebrant® with certification in Weddings. She lives in Birmingham, Michigan. Kim can be reached by email at kimnash2@aol.com.

Remembering Our Roots

IVY COX

On the first and fifteenth of every lunar month, many residents of Taiwan set up an altar and adorn it with candles and offerings of food, rice wine, and incense in honor of their ancestors. By adopting this ritual to honor your own ancestors, you can strengthen your connection to your own past and gain resources for the present.

MATERIALS

Mementos from ancestors

PREPARATION

You may want to select significant dates on which to honor your ancestors. Or, you may choose to honor them whenever you think of them. Set aside a place of honor in your home, one that you can dedicate to the memory of your ancestors. Make sure the space is not cluttered by other items such as keys or loose change.

IN MEMORY

- Hold the memento(s) in your hand.

- Then take a deep breath, close your eyes, and think good thoughts with every fiber of your being.

    — You may wish your ancestors well.

    — You may request a blessing.

    — You may reflect on your family history.

- When you are done, open your eyes slowly. Perhaps smile.

IN CLOSING

While the ritual of honoring ancestors with incense and altars may at first seem foreign, the idea is universal. No matter where we are from, it is meaningful to connect with ancestors who have helped to shape who we are. You will find yourself more content in the present when you can rest secure in having honored your past.

IVY COX, is a Life-Cycle Celebrant with certification in Weddings. She lives in New Jersey with her husband, two kids, and a Boston terrier. Ivy can be reached by email at ivy.cox@gmail.com.

Building Families with Sand

LOIS HECKMAN

As a Life-Cycle Celebrant® it is my job, my calling, and my honor to create wonderful ceremonies for life's big milestones. Most folks have no idea how to incorporate their kids, but transitions such as weddings and baby blessings are big days not only for those being ritualized, but also for the children in a family. A family sand ceremony is a clear, simple, and beautiful ritual element that works for children of all ages.

MATERIALS

- Ceremony table

- Larger container in which to pour sand

- Small containers, each holding a particular color of sand for each participant

Invite participants to choose the color of sand that will represent them. Look up the symbolism behind each color and meditate on how that symbolism applies to each participant.

THE SAND CEREMONY

The sand ceremony makes concrete and active a process of blending and change that is happening in a family's life. As you hand containers of sand to participants, speak to the different qualities that each participant brings to the event.

- Have each participant take a turn pouring a portion of sand into the container.

- Repeat the process until all individual containers have been emptied.

IN CLOSING

It's a real-life rainbow, the blend that is a family. Working together, family members can create something bigger and even more beautiful than each individual.

Lois Heckman is a full-time certified Life-Cycle Celebrant® who was a pioneer of the profession. She and her husband of 35 years have created an outdoor ceremony site in the Pocono Mountains, where she performs weddings. Lois can be reached through her website, www.loisheckman.com.

Strategies for Child-Friendly Celebrations

CINDY MATCHETT

Children love to be in community. They love to wear special clothes and have special jobs and be a part of something important and meaningful. But they can also get tired, shy, over-stimulated, hungry, and cranky from trying to handle the big energy of ceremonies. Here are some excellent strategies for smoothing that energy into something they can handle.

PREPARATION

Whether they're ring-bearers or flower girls, honorees at a birthday or blessing, or simply guests at a family reunion, children thrive when they are accepted for who and where they are in their development—and when their grownups stay a few steps ahead of them!

CROSS-CEREMONY TIPS FOR BECOMING CHILD-FRIENDLY

- For a ceremony honoring a child, choose a time of day that best supports the child's rhythm.

- Practice. Your little one is probably very excited—and a little nervous—about the special event, particularly if he or she has an assigned part to play. A fun rehearsal with props can be very helpful.

- Have loved ones close by, so this is whom the child sees.

- Build in break times, with a healthy snack, a diaper change, or a potty break. Let the party continue as you take a slow, sacred breath together.

- Keep it short and sweet. Plan on ending (or leaving) while everyone's still having fun.

- Relax and go with the flow. If your child decides, even at the last minute, that it's all too much for him or her, accept it, explain to others, and move on.

IN CLOSING

A child is a blessing at any ceremony, so relax, drop your fears, and simply be present. Your sense of humor and acceptance will be an added blessing for all.

Cindy Matchett is a Life-Cycle Celebrant® with certification in Weddings and Ceremonies Across the Life Cycle. She lives with her family in an old schoolhouse outside of Boston. Cindy can be reached through her website, www.meaningfulcelebrations.com.

Magical, not Mundane

DANA M. ZIPKIN

As a mom to three children under the age of six, I grew to appreciate those daily rituals that seem so ordinary: preparing breakfast, going to the park after school, reading a story before bedtime. They provide a comfortable routine, and even more importantly, a positive impact on relationships among everyone in the household. Each day-to-day ritual provides us with an opportunity to celebrate being a family and to recognize that we are loved and needed, a much-welcomed experience given the inevitable push-and-pull of life. The following daily experiences seem to be especially powerful for my family.

DAILY RITUALS

- Wake-up Call. One of my daughters is an early riser, so my husband and I have given her the role of "human alarm clock." She knocks on doors, gently tells us it's time to get out of bed, and asks if we've slept well. Her older sister and younger brother adore these few minutes with her. It's a wonderful way to start the day with smiles instead of scowls!

- Post-Dinner Song and Dance. We fire up the iPod, sing along to our favorite songs, and dance like fools. Everyone chats and laughs and shakes off whatever stress the day might have caused.

- Storytime Twist. Most bedtimes in our home begin with the reading of a story or two. Every once in a while, though, we create original stories that require everyone's input in order to get to the end. Characters are developed, plot lines thicken, and creativity flows. It's an excellent way to close the day.

IN CLOSING

Ritual denotes actions performed mainly for their symbolic value. In our case, the symbolism is clearly expressed through the joy we derive from these everyday tasks; they embody the fabric of our family. My second-born recently summed it up best: "I love hanging out with you guys because it's like magic that makes me happy!"

DANA M. ZIPKIN is a Life-Cycle Celebrant® with certification in Weddings, Funerals, and Ceremonies Across the Life Cycle. She lives in northern New Jersey with her husband and their three children. Dana can be reached by email at dana@ceremoniesbydana.com or through her website, www.ceremoniesbydana.com.

How to Honor the Elders in Your Family

DIANE GANSAUER

In April 2012, my family was discussing the upcoming 98th birthday of our Aunt Helen, who survived the Great Depression and tended the home front while her three brothers fought for our country in World War II. We agreed that we shouldn't wait to honor Helen but should instead pay tribute to her while she was able to enjoy the moment.

PREPARATION

I started calling Helen to listen to her stories. She'd start out by saying that she wasn't feeling very well, but before long it was hard to keep up with all the memories that poured out of her. By the fall, I had printed a mini-biography that Helen could edit.

Here's how we prepared for the tribute dinner:

- I wrote a simple ceremony on the theme of "the family tree."

- A family member brought a beautiful hand-drawn family tree tracing our heritage back to the 1500s.

- We booked a banquet room and placed on each table a small tree on which people could hang notes to Helen.

- We set a table with photos of family members who had passed away and gave thanks for their presence in our lives.

- Each person was given a card extolling the example trees provide by sinking roots into the ground and by changing with the seasons.

- The youngest children brought small gifts to give Helen.

THE TRIBUTE

On Helen's big night, family members gathered at a banquet room near her home. We shared mealtime grace and named loved ones who could not make the journey. And then my husband gave a funny speech that put Helen's life in historical context: "Aunt Helen has outlasted almost everything from the Austro-Hungarian Empire to Phyllis Diller." Then family members took turns reading parts of Helen's poignant and funny story out loud.

Later that evening, when she heard her favorite big band music, Helen led the dancing. When she looked around and said, "They all came!" I knew we had not only honored her but had also given her—and the whole family—a very happy memory.

IN CLOSING

There is no simpler, more beautiful way to honor someone than to make room for their story to be told. By listening, we affirm the one who lived the story and we protect it from being lost. As time goes on, questions and observations by the youngest family members reveal that they are keeping these family stories in their hearts.

DIANE GANSAUER is a Life-Cycle Celebrant® with certification in Funerals and Ceremonies Across the Life Cycle. She lives in the foothills of Evergreen, Colorado, with her husband, Bob. Diane can be reached by email at diane@lyricallifeceremonies.com or through her website, www.lyricallifeceremonies.com.

Celebrate Your Canine Companions

ANNEMARIE JUHLIAN

Yes, I'm one of those crazy dog lovers. My husband and I have a household of older and special-needs dogs, all rescued from neglect and abuse. In my work as a celebrant, I have found that creating everyday celebrations around the dogs in my life brings me great peace and joy. If you are an animal lover, here are few simple one-step rituals to celebrate and honor your beloved canine or other animal companion:

ONE-STEP RITUALS

- Candle Lighting. Each morning, I light a candle and ask the invisible world to come to the aid of neglected, abused and abandoned companion animals and farm animals. By sending out a little grace each morning on behalf of animals, I feel blessed to be connected to a higher source and vision for what may be.

- Morning Tea/Coffee. Each morning, I take one of our dogs and sit on the couch with a cup of tea and have "doggie quiet time." Some mornings it may be just five minutes. Other mornings, it could be 30 minutes. This is my ritual time to "be," an art mastered by the dogs in my life.

- Wish Box. Many years ago, I created a "wish box" to serve as a touchstone for requests and blessings around the animals in my life. Whenever I hear of a dog in need of rescue or healing, I write a request and put it in the box, asking that a highest intention be served. Often I am astonished by what happens.

- Painted Portrait. If you have a special animal in your life, consider having an artist paint a special picture of your sweet one. When you glance up, you will see a portrait to help you focus on what is important in your life.

IN CLOSING

No matter what your faith, spiritual path, or tradition, the art and joy of having a dog or other animal companion is a daily wonder that can be intentionally celebrated. At the end of the day with our dogs, it's all about love. We and our animals all benefit from intentionally creating "time out" rituals to honor our canine companions.

Annemarie Juhlian is a Life-Cycle Celebrant® with certification in Wedding and Funerals. She and her husband, Greg, reside on beautiful Bainbridge Island, a short ferry ride from Seattle, Washington, with their family of special needs and rescue dogs. Annemarie can be reached at anne@marriedbyannemarie.com or through her website, www.marriedbyannemarie.com.

"Be yourself;

EVERYONE ELSE

IS already TAKEN"

— Oscar Wilde

CHAPTER 5

Personal Growth

The passenger should always fit his or her own mask before helping children, the disabled, or persons requiring assistance.

People who are oriented toward nurturing, supporting, and helping others often find it difficult to embark upon self-care. We plan to initiate a practice, only to get bogged down in choosing a path. Or we may decide to put off self-care until everyone else is doing well, only to find there is always someone needing help.

The irony is that a centered, happy, well cared for individual is much, much better at providing direction, support, and sustenance to others. Walking our own path centers us and lends us strength and peace. It also gives us insight into the obstacles and rewards that others face on their own personal path.

It can take very little time to check in with yourself now and then, and there are so many ways to do it! The following ceremonies offer a multitude of opportunities to support your own personal growth.

Kim Kirkley paves the way by offering practical support for living our lives from a standpoint of love instead of fear. Gail Fern Peekeekoot offers a mnemonic to help douse the flames of fear. AC Warden suggests cultivation methods for the soul. Janna Henning models ways to restore equilibrium at the end of a taxing day. And, mindful that we all get lost sometimes, Sacha Jones suggests a variety of ways to reset intentions.

Dorry Bless reminds us how to celebrate the small stuff. And, speaking of small stuff, Marta Adubato shows how to learn from the pets in our lives.

Together, these ceremonies by celebrants who walk the walk offer sustenance and renewal, not only in preparation for life's big moments, but also toward mindful living every day.

Morning Happiness Ritual

KIM KIRKLEY

As a little girl, did you beg for a pet lizard? And, when you finally got to bring lovely Lizzie the Lizard home, did you cuddle with her for hours? I didn't think so.

Yet, you got one. We all have a reptile in our brains—the part of the brain that is dedicated to fear. We share this bit of biology with reptiles, and when we lived a primitive way of life, it was the perfect tool for helping us recognize and overcome the physical threats to our survival. However these days most of our challenges are not physical. We rarely need to outrun our opponents. Instead, we need to out-love them! In our modern world, virtually every difficulty we face can be overcome by being more loving. When we choose to bring more love to a situation we choose to be happy. Every morning, we can remind ourselves to forget the reptile in our brains and move forward in love.

PREPARATION

The moments when you first awaken include some of your most precious and important opportunities to set the tone for the day. Resolve to give them to your best self, not your reptile.

MORNING HAPPINESS

- Spend your first five, fifteen, or sixty minutes focusing on loving good thoughts. Pray or meditate, reminding yourself of the love you embody. Stand or sit with your eyes closed and your attention centered in your heart and give thanks for life.

- While thinking of whatever challenge you face, ask, *how can I bring more love to this situation?* This form of focusing can help you rise into the transformative love of your neocortex, instead of reacting primitively, like a reptile, to the challenges you face.

CONTINUING THE HAPPINESS RITUAL

There is no closing...this work is never done. Choose love!

Kim Kirkley is a full-time certified Life-Cycle Celebrant® who was a pioneer of the profession. She lives and works in the New York City metropolitan area. Kim can be reached through any of her websites, www.ourelegantceremony.com, www.elegantgaynywedding.com, or www.lifestoryfuneralnyc.com.

Stop, Drop, & Roll!

GAIL FERN PEEKEEKOOT

It can be next to impossible to miss the fear-inducing messages bombarding us. It takes a little more effort to find the messages of those engaged in the collective work of conscious evolution, those who believe the tide of great positive change for humanity has already turned, way down deep, and that our current crisis is preceding a great evolutionary jump.

PUTTING OUT THE FIRE

Until humanity can see that the tide has indeed turned, we will likely need to get through our own fears and be ready to help others cope with theirs. With that intention in mind, I offer this three-part ritual. It is 100-percent personally tested.

- Stop! Unless you are in immediate physical danger (in which case, please feel free to skip this whole ritual), stop! As soon as you sense the smoky tendrils of fear winding through your mind, stop the flow of negative thought and override it with a prayer, mantra, chant, or song. The prayer I use comes from Julian of Norwich: "All shall be well and all shall be well and all manner of thing shall be well." However, even "Row, Row, Row Your Boat" could work.

- Once you have settled your thoughts and are living fully in the present moment (rather than the regret-filled past or fear-filled future) focus on something that makes you smile. Personally, I picture a pile of warm puppies.

- Drop! As you smile, drop your awareness from your head into your heart. Take a few good, deep breaths.

- When you are ready, become aware of the stillness and unconditional love within and around you. Fake it 'til you feel it! It's there.

- Surround the fear-invoking situation with unconditional love and compassion and set an intention for the best outcome for all.

- Hold that intention as you picture yourself standing in a waterfall, releasing the fear and any other uncomfortable emotions to be carried away and transformed.

IN CLOSING

- Roll! Before you return to daily life, have a big drink of water and go for a brisk walk to clear the cortisol out of your brain.

- Then, following your own inner guidance, roll on.

GAIL FERN PEEKEEKOOT is a Life-Cycle Celebrant® with certification in Funerals. She lives on Vancouver Island, in Canada. Gail can be reached through her website, www.riteintentions.com.

Hit Your Personal Reset Button

SACHA JONES

You may frequently hit the reset button on a lot of trendy gadgets, but there is one piece of valuable equipment that is guaranteed to last a lifetime if you reset it regularly. That valuable piece of equipment is . . . you!

PREPARATION

- Hydration, hydration, hydration! Starting your day with a big glass of filtered tap water will rev up your body and help you start your day fresh.

- Stretch and Breathe. When you get up in the morning, do what your pet does: stretch! Inhale love and positivity and exhale all those things you don't need.

- Keep a journal. Ask yourself, *Why do I want to reset my wellness button? How will I go about doing this?*

- "Altar" your world. Clear a spot on your desk, a shelf, even a side table, and make a mini-altar in praise of the changes you are making.

- Switch it up. Get rid of your daily coffee ritual and introduce yourself to delicious herbal teas. Let go of people who don't help you grow and seek out those who want to see you blossom.

- Plant a plant. To watch something grow is to witness transformation.

IN CLOSING

Relish the feeling of freedom from habits, fears, or toxicity, and reintroduce yourself to the things that nourish your heart, mind, body, and soul.

SACHA JONES is a Life-Cycle Celebrant® with certification in Weddings. She lives in New York City's East Village. Sacha can be reached by email at sachajonesceremonies@gmail. com or through her website, www.stiggly.com.

Lead with Your Dominant Paw!

MARTA K. ADUBATO

Oh, the possibilities! I have learned much over the years from my relationships with felines, including my gorgeous Bengal cat, Margaret. When Margaret checks out something new, she always leads with her left front paw. She trusts her instincts and pulls back when the path or item is dangerous—or uninteresting! As someone who is still learning from her four-legged, cold-nose-kiss-giving, wise, and ever-inquisitive Bengal cat, I suggest the following ritual as a simple but powerful way to take the first step toward completing the unfinished sentences in our lives.

PREPARATION

Choose a doorway in your home and stand outside it. Are you planning healthier eating? Choose the kitchen doorway. Are you looking to start a new business? Choose the doorway to your office or the room that could become an office. Are you looking for intimacy? Choose the bedroom door. You get the idea!

LEAD WITH YOUR DOMINANT PAW

- Close your eyes; breathe in and then out.

- Imagine the possibility you long to have happen. Even if you don't have the entire picture, imagine that you do. Breathe in and then out again.

- Dominant foot first, step over the threshold. Say out loud, "I have taken the hardest step, the first one."

- Open your eyes and congratulate yourself on having taken that first step!

IN CLOSING

Believe that you are on your way to a new adventure and the best time of your life. The world before you, become what Norman Vincent Peale called a "possibilitarian." Lead with your dominant paw!

MARTA K. ADUBATO is a Life-Cycle Celebrant® with certification in Weddings, Funerals, and Ceremonies Across the Life Cycle. Marta lives in Central Indiana with her husband, a dog, and four cats. She can be reached by email at m.adubato@yahoo.com or through her website, www.waitingtobetold.net.

Restore and Refresh the Spirit

JANNA HENNING

PREPARATION

I use ritual to close and cleanse my workspace at the end of each day. I mindfully tidy my office, rinsing out teacups, emptying garbage cans, and straightening items on the coffee table to make room for a fresh, clean start. As I clean, I ritually note the ways my clients and I have grown and changed and how my work has made a difference in their lives. I place physical reminders of these successes, such as letters, photographs, and collages, in a purple folder for regular review.

At the end of the week I take a few moments to burn sage in my office in order to neutralize and move old, spent energy in the space. The scent of sage also is a sensory reminder of the transition into rest. As I turn off the lights and close the door, I pause to take these visual cues into my awareness and gently remind myself that the time for work has ended and the time for rest and replenishment has begun.

RESTORING AND REFRESHING THE SPIRIT

- I walk home slowly, feeling the movement of my muscles and the support of the ground beneath my feet. Grounding brings me back to the here and now. I take care to notice the sensory world: the temperature of the air, plant and animal life, and sounds from near and far.

- At home, I feed my senses by petting my cats, taking a warm bath, wearing comfortable clothing, drinking a soothing beverage, and eating healthy and delicious food.

- After I've fully transitioned to full body awareness, I take note of my emotional state. After attending all day to others, I ask myself what I need. Do I need a good laugh, playfulness, and silliness? Or would an exchange of affection or support be more helpful? Awareness of my own needs helps me seek support from loved ones and brings me back to my enduring relationships.

IN CLOSING

Author Tom Attig has called the spirit "the soaring aspect of our will to live," including growth, hope, and meaning. Restoring your own spirit gives you strength you can then share with others.

JANNA HENNING is a Life-Cycle Celebrant® with certification in Funerals. She lives in Chicago. Janna can be reached by email at janna.henning@gmail.com.

Cultivating Your Soul's Potential

AC WARDEN

Those of us who garden or farm celebrate summer as a season of cultivation. As the earth heats up and our garden plots develop, we enjoy spring lettuce, asparagus, rhubarb, celery, beets, and onions—the fruits of our labors. Small flowers appear on our tomato and squash plants, and we can imagine how abundant our harvest will be in fall. All this happens because we take the time to prepare the soil and to cultivate and nurture seeds. We can enjoy the same kind of harvest for our souls if we take the time and prepare the way. The following simple steps can help you to cultivate and nurture your inner resources.

MATERIALS
- Paper
- Pen or pencil

PREPARATION
You can do this ritual with a group of friends or by yourself. If you are with a group, you can sit together in a circle. Find a quiet place, indoors or outdoors, where you won't be interrupted for about twenty minutes.

NURTURING YOUR SOUL
- On a piece of paper write a single intention for growth. Choose any area of personal growth you would like to see for yourself. You can write that you intend to be a better listener, or that you intend not to let an addiction or anger overwhelm you, or that you'll complete a project or become active in an organization.

- Share your intentions or say them out loud so that you can hear them resonate.

- Then close your eyes and visualize yourself with intentions fulfilled. Imagine yourself listening; or living without anger; or working on that project you have put off for too long.

- Breathe.

IN CLOSING

Remember, cultivation is joyful but it takes time. Do this exercise once a week for twenty minutes though, and watch for the harvest to come.

AC WARDEN is a Life-Cycle Celebrant® with certification in Weddings, Funerals, and Ceremonies for Healing. She lives and practices in the DMV (District of Columbia, Maryland, and Virginia). AC can be reached by email at acwarden@capitalceremonies.com or through her website, www.capitalceremonies.com

Celebrate the Ordinarius

DORRY BLESS

The adjective ordinary dates back to the fourteenth century French word *ordinarie* and the Latin word *ordinarius*, meaning "customary, regular, usual and orderly." In the age of Facebook, 24/7 media, reality shows, YouTube, blogs, and Twitter, being recognized for something—anything—is incredibly seductive. The truth is, however, that we spend most of our lives in ordinary time. And it's in ordinary time that most awakenings occur. Ordinary time invites us to develop a way of being that is a simple, constant practice.

PREPARATION FOR AWAKENING

This is some of the wonder and magic of living Life Ordinarius:

- Yesterday, while on a very long line to get my car washed, it quickly became apparent that it would take at least one hour to accomplish this task. It dawned on me that I didn't have to use this time wisely. Instead, I could just wait. I could do nothing, and so I did.

- After my computer technician lost my contacts and calendar while reformatting my hard drive, I became convinced I needed to upgrade to a smart phone. Then I realized my phone works just fine and is smart enough for me.

- Since my husband has multiple sclerosis, he has had to develop a new way of walking. The guy who once jumped out of planes and literally carried me up the wedding aisle progresses with something between a shuffle and a deliberate, slow motion dance. Sometimes he gets his momentum going and needs a wall to stop him. Still, I can't help but appreciate his new inimitable style.

THE ROOT AWAKENING

Begin by planting your feet on the earth just like a big, sprawling tree. Allow yourself to sink into the ground of being that connects us all. Drop your awareness down into your feet. Wiggle your toes. Notice that roots have no leaves, that they store food and nutrients, and that they anchor themselves to another plant if necessary. Wake up to your own rootedness. Discover what that is for you.

IN CLOSING

Every time you see a tree, let it wake you up to the mystery of your life. See what it feels like to live life from the ground up. What does it do to your perspective? It might just mean that in the big picture roots of change are afoot!

DORRY BLESS is a Life-Cycle Celebrant® with certification in Weddings, Funerals, and Ceremonies Across the Life Cycle. She lives a stone's throw from the Musconetcong River in New Jersey with her husband, daughter, and two dogs. Dorry can be reached by email at dorry@circleoffifeceremonies. com or through her website, www.circleoflifeceremonies.com.

You, Incorporated

SHERI REDA

In this age of big business, the term *incorporated* may bring to mind the capitalist process of building a legal entity. In business, corporations limit personal responsibility by standing in the place of the real people that run them. From the standpoint of pure language, however, to incorporate is to bring parts in, to make them part of the body. The daily ritual that follows can set the tone for the day and contextualize your encounters as teachings and gifts.

MATERIALS

Bring to your meditation space or breakfast table elements that symbolize sources of strength. You might use the following materials, adding additional items that speak to you:

- Candle, for light, heat and/or smoke

- Food, for nourishment

- Fruit, for an ethic of appreciation

- Incense, potpourri, or flowers, to remind you to open all your senses

- Media—music, print, or electronic—reminders to learn and to share

- Water, coffee, or tea, as a reminder of resources all around you

INCORPORATION CEREMONY

- As you bring each ritual element to your space, evoke mindfulness by saying the name of the item. Then, seat your self among these symbolic virtues of each day, every day.

- Touch each item and incorporate it, literally, into your sensory life in the way that feels most appropriate to you. For example, you might gaze at the candlelight, inhale the smoke, or feel the power of lighting the candle or blowing it out.

- Make a positive statement about bringing the qualities of the item into your general approach to life or into a moment that may call for a particular quality.

- Step back from the enactment of high ritual and enjoy breakfast, aware that you are incorporating into your experience and your very body the qualities you have discerned this day.

IN CLOSING

It's easy to refresh your ritual experience throughout the day. Glance up at the overhead lights and remember the candle you consecrated earlier in the day. Sip your midmorning coffee and recall the sense memory of your breakfast drink. Touch some common item and give a thought to its admirable qualities. And find something to love in every little thing, all day.

SHERI REDA is a Mster Life-Cycle Celebrant® with certification in Weddings, Funerals, Ceremonies Across the Life Cycle, and Ceremonies for Healing. She lives in Chicago with her husband and the younger of her two great kids. Sheri can be reached by email at sheri.a.reda@gmail.com or through her website, www.flowceremonies.com.

"I DWELL IN possibility"

— Emily Dickinson

CHAPTER 6
Honoring Transitions

Grief is a funny, loyal kind of thing. It comes to us when we suffer almost any kind of loss. We expect and honor the grief that accompanies the death of a family member, friend, or neighbor. We are supported, then, in stepping back from our life patterns, expressing sadness, and pondering a new future.

But grief can surprise us unaware sometimes. We may resent it when something sad happens and we want to move on. We might reject it, fight it, hold it at bay as an unwelcome guest during happy life transitions. Yet every transition remakes our world, and every kind of change—even happy exciting change—entails loss. It can be important to acknowledge and express all the emotions that go into big life changes. To both mourn the old and celebrate the new. To both honor our fears and support our highest hopes.

These ceremonies offer myriad ways to do just that. In this chapter, Lara Vesta observes the constant that we call change. She reminds us of many ways to experience the love and support that surround us always. To honor the mixed emotions that come along with growing old, Holly Pruett offers a birthday celebration that is also a ceremony of letting go. Amanda German and Stacy Mitchell give us ways to honor "silent" losses such as miscarriage and stillbirth.

Yet grief isn't all that comes to us with change. Every ending brings a new beginning. Carol Takacs suggests a ceremony to mark and make mindful those new beginnings in a minor key. She encourages us to note and celebrate that growing friendship or that new perspective. And Robyn Greene goes one further. Her suggestions help us acknowledge and honor the mini-transitions that move us from minute to minute throughout the day.

Every moment that ends heralds a new moment beginning. These ceremonies help us ring out the old and ring in the new.

A Circle of Strength

LARA VESTA

Transition is a constant. We are all in transition, but there are times when we feel the changes more strongly. In such times, we can draw upon the strength of our ancestors, real and imagined. When we feel unsettled or unloved, we can root into what grounds us, what we love to practice, believe, or do. We can invoke the qualities we wish to embody from within a circle of strength and set intentions for transition to the next phase of life. This circle of strength can remind you of where you come from, who you are, and what you wish to be.

MATERIALS

Walk through your home, gathering images or objects that remind you of strength, personal power, and joy. Include objects that represent what you want or need to do in order to feel whole. You might select seeds from a garden, a stone from the beach, a quote, or a note of praise from a colleague of friend. Let your intuition guide your collection of objects and symbols; you can always think later about what they represent to you.

PREPARATION

Give yourself some time to be alone and select a space where you won't be disturbed.

SURROUNDING YOURSELF WITH SUPPORT

- Craft a circle of objects and images on the floor or ground, arranging the objects and images in a way that pleases you.

- Step into the circle.

- Breathe. Feel the steadiness of the earth beneath you. Allow yourself time to observe what surrounds you.

- Sit for a while in calmness. When you feel ready you may stand and exit.

CLOSING

If you can, keep the circle around for a bit in some form. For example, the objects you used might grace a shelf or an altar. Take time each day to visit the objects and write an affirmation of strength. You might imagine a letter from one of your ancestors. What could they say to you about your power? I imagine, always, the women who came before me saying, "You come from us. We live within you. You are strong."

LARA VESTA is a Life-Cycle Celebrant® with certification in Ceremonies Across the Life Cycle. She lives on the banks of the Willamette River in Portland, Oregon, with her family. Lara can be reached by email at lara@laravesta.com or through her website, www.laravesta.com.

Mini-Transitions

ROBYN GREENE

Many people are familiar with the term circadian rhythms, which are the twenty-four hour patterns by which most beings live, but most have not heard of ultradian rhythms. Ultradian rhythms are the ninety-minute cycles by which we experience energy and fatigue.

Most of us try to fight these rhythms. We drink coffee and try to plow through tasks no matter how long it takes or how we feel. But preliminary studies show that people who observe their need for a break—and take that break—actually wind up getting more done. So why not give the day's transitions their due?

PREPARATION

You might want to begin upon waking, which is, after all, the day's first transition. Before you start going madly through your day, sit a few moments and clear the mental decks. Ask for guidance or just think about something you value about yourself.

ONE-STEP WAYS TO HONOR TRANSITIONS

- Whenever you notice your energy start to drag, put down what you are doing and breathe. Focus your attention on both the inhalation and the exhalation, allowing the exhalation to be a bit longer.

- Do some stretching and then take a short walk.

- Meditate or listen to some peaceful music that you enjoy.

- As you shift activities, note where you last were and what you last did. Then let it go. Affirm for yourself that you are shifting your consciousness toward something new.

IN CLOSING

Recently I was in the Loire Valley, in France, where a church at the center of town rang bells on the hour and half hour. At one time, people organized their time around those bells. They literally tolled the time. If you listen carefully, your body will tell you too. Every ninety minutes, it tells you that it's time to let go.

ROBYN GREENE is a Life-Cycle Celebrant® with certification in Weddings. Robyn has lived in the San Francisco Bay Area since 1976. She can be reached by email at rofree@att.net.

A Ritual for New Beginnings

CAROL TAKACS

The big transitions in life such as graduation, marriage, the birth of a child, or the launch of a business are like raw pieces of cloth. The smaller passages, such as the development of a new friendship or a new way of looking at a challenge, are like the thread that binds the cloth together. Both kinds of passages are important in creating the fabric of our lives. To honor them, I invite you to partake in this ceremony for new beginnings.

MATERIALS

Elements from nature

PREPARATION

- Recite an intention for the ceremony.

- Bring the elements from nature into your ceremony by lighting a candle (fire), sipping a cup of tea (water), feeling the earth beneath your feet (earth), and taking three deep, restorative breaths (air).

- Play a recording of music that reflects your mood.

CEREMONY

- Sit quietly or move to the music you are playing.

- Reflect on the journey you've embarked upon. What brought you to this moment? What do you envision for the future? What are your hopes? Honor feelings that come up.

- Select a symbol that represents this beginning. Symbols may include seeds representing a new life emerging, a rock signifying strength, a flower showing the beauty of this beginning, a butterfly embodying the journey you are taking.

- State your intentions or recitie a prayer or poem.

IN CLOSING

My passion for new beginnings comes from the energy of renewal and hope that a new beginning sparks within. When you are faced with a new beginning, make a special place for it in the tapestry of life. The energy and renewal it brings will help you make the most of your new start.

CAROL TAKACS is a Life-Cycle Celebrant® with certification in Funerals. Carol lives in Connecticut. She can be reached by email at carol@yourlifecelebrated.com or through her website, www.yourlifecelebrated.com.

Loss and a Snowflake

AMANDA GERMAN

In December 2002, I became joyously pregnant with our first child. But only a few months later, the world around me seemed to blur. Cramping, bleeding, and the words from the ER doctor filled my space: "You're having a miscarriage."

Years have passed since that tragic event. Two children and two additional miscarriages have filled my womb and our family since then. Yet that first pregnancy remains an indelible experience. As the snow began to fall this morning, I gazed at the intricate, kaleidoscopic balance of order and disorder descending to Earth. I gathered some materials and began to construct my own snowflake in a restorative ritual that others who have experienced loss, including miscarriage or loss of a child, might consider as well.

MATERIALS

- Paper
- Scissors

PREPARATION

I cut a sheet of paper into a circle. Next, I folded the paper circle in half. Then I halved the sheet of paper three more times.

THE SNOWFLAKE

I envisioned what this snowflake would look like, much as I had envisioned my first child. Then I picked up the scissors and began.

- Precisely and carefully, I began making cuts, considering how each choice I made during the snowflake's creation would alter its future.

- Soon the paper cone in my hand was full of intricate shapes. All of the little pieces lying before me were part of the whole. I scooped up the pieces, piled them to the side, and continued to cut.

- Finally, with anticipation, I opened my snowflake and reflected on every snowflake's fleeting journey. I noted that they do not fall alone. Finding a warm spot, some of them melt, leaving behind only a small drop of water like a tear.

IN CLOSING

As a woman, wife, daughter, and mother, my life has changed again and again—but never more than that first time. The images of the snowflakes I made remind me to see the beauty in it all. My pile of pieces became an image of what my snowflake of a pregnancy had left behind. It was as beautiful as the snowflake itself. Both framed creations now hang in my home alongside a copy of Emily Warburton's poem entitled "Each of Us a Snowflake."

AMANDA GERMAN is a Life-Cycle Celebrant® with certification in Ceremonies Across the Life Cycle. She lives in Anchorage, Alaska, with her husband of fifteen years and two great boys. Amanda can be reached by email at silylilmnky@yahoo.com.

Honoring the Silent Loss

STACY MITCHELL

Although miscarriage in the first trimester is one of the most common as well as one of the most emotionally powerful losses for a woman or couple to experience, it is often a silent loss. The emotional and physical pain can be intense; yet speaking about the loss is often taboo. This common, silent approach may you get back to ordinary life, but it does nothing to honor the life potential you experienced or the loss you suffered. The following rituals, however, are ways you can mark your experience.

ONE-STEP RITUALS FOR LOSS

- In some cultures our hair is said to hold our memories and experiences. Consider cutting your hair to honor your transition. You can donate it to a charity, give it to birds to build nests, or make a locket or other memento.

- Begin or resume a practice of tai chi, yoga, Pilates, or other breath/energy work that involves movement and flow to place yourself back in your body.

- Write out your story, journal your feelings, or create something in a medium of your choice that serves to release your emotions.

- Designate or create a song to memorialize the child lost.

- Take a ritual nature walk or do a walking meditation and take something from or give something to the universe as you go. A feather, rock, shell, or other natural item can symbolize release and renewal.

- Consider the ritual release of butterflies or a sunset sky lantern.

- Plant a tree, shrub, or flower, and make a ritual practice of nourishing your plants. If you have kept blood from the miscarriage or your first menstrual cycle afterward, you may wish to bury it in the soil near your plant.

- Build a fire and release to it bits of paper that carry your thoughts and feelings.

- Hold a women's circle or a family circle of people who are supportive of you in your loss. Speak if you want to, have a ritual meal with favorite foods, or simply enjoy the company of people you love.

IN CLOSING

The miscarriage process is often very introspective. A woman who suffers this physical and emotional loss should be in complete control of any rituals she wishes to use and who, if anyone, she wants involved in the process.

STACY MITCHELL is a Life-Cycle Celebrant® with certification in Funerals and Ceremonies for Healing. Stacy lives on the central coast of California with her husband and family. She can be reached by email at celebrant@honoryourvoice.com or through website, www.honoryourvoice.com.

Letting Go into the River of Life

HOLLY PRUETT

As I approached my fiftieth birthday, I knew I wanted a ritual that would go deeper than the typical big blow-out party. So I planned a ceremony that would honor the flow of my life and the ways it merges with the life streams of all those around me.

MATERIALS

- Blue ribbons
- Candles
- Photographs
- Symbolic gifts for and from each guest

PREPARATION

- Meditate to clarify your image of the river of life. Ask yourself what a river means to you. Where are you on the river's journey? What streams are converging? Is the current swift and the mood adventurous? Is it treacherous, calm, or cleansing?

- Journal your thoughts and work with them until you have a clear vision for the ceremony you want to create.

- Invite participants of many ages, including, if possible, at least one guest from each decade of life. Ask each guest to bring a symbol of his or her present age.

- Designate a ceremonial space using pebbles, candles, leaves, or other objects meaningful to you.

- Lay down a ribbon of deep blue representing the river of time, and place an unlit tea light candle representing each participant at an interval along the ribbon.

- Place a photo or object from an ancestor at one end and a baby photo of yourself closer to the other.

THE CEREMONY

- Open the ceremony with a focusing act, such as burning sage or sounding a chime, and offer each participant a personal welcome.

- Light a candle and place it on the scarf. Then invite each guest, from the youngest to the eldest, to set down a symbol, light a candle, and take a gift representing their role in your life.

- When you have reached the end of the river, listen to or sing a song such as "Peace of the River," by Glendora Gosling and Viola Wood.

IN CLOSING

Close the ceremonial circle by burning squares of tissue paper inscribed with anything you wish to release. Then embark on some kind of feast and celebrate your day!

HOLLY PRUETT is a Life-Cycle Celebrant with certification in Funerals and Ceremonies Across the Life Cycle. She lives in Portland, Oregon, with her life partner, Amber, and their two cats. Holly can be reached by email at holly@hollypruettcelebrant.com or through her website, www.hollypruettcelebrant.com.

Charlotte Eulette is a Certified Life-Cycle Celebrant® who has served as the International Executive Director and spokesperson for the Celebrant Foundation & Institute since the inception in 2001. Charlotte has published articles about the importance of personalized ceremonies in *American Funeral Director*, *Natural Awakenings*, and *Spirituality and Health* and has been interviewed on BBC Radio and on NPR's *All Things Considered* and *Marketwatch*. She has appeared on NBC and CNN News as well as *This Morning and News with Dan Rather* on CBS. Charlotte is married and lives in beautiful New Jersey with her family. Her email address is charlotteeulette@celebrantinstitute.org.

Sheri Reda is a Master Life-Cycle Celebrant® dedicated to creating one-of-a-kind ceremonies honoring all of life's milestones. She is also a certified spiritual director, holding space for people in the process of spiritual discovery. Sheri loves words almost as much as she loves people so she also writes stories, essays, and poems, and sometimes performs them. She frequently works as a librarian and often contributes to textbooks. Sheri and her family live in Chicago and Los Angeles. Her email address is sherireda@flowceremonies.com.

Sarah Lemp is a Certified Life-Cycle Celebrant® who has been creating and leading weddings, baby blessings, first moon rites, and spiritual empowerment and healing rituals since 2000. She enjoys infusing ceremonies with crystals, aromatherapy, and herbal elements whenever appropriate. Sarah earned her BA in Graphic Design from American University. She is a lifelong spiritual seeker and creative spirit who loves to cook, crochet, knit, camp, hike, sew, and make homemade bath and body products. Sarah lives in California with her husband Chris. Sarah's email address is sarah@sarahmony.com.